D1555477

How To Color PHOTOGRAPHS WITH OILS

BY

W. J. SEEMANN

VER HALEN PUBLICATIONS
6060 SUNSET BOULEVARD
HOLLYWOOD 28, CALIFORNIA

ILLUSTRATIONS

Illustrations Colored by the Author

CONTENTS

C O N T E N T S—*(Cont.)*

FIRST PRINTING — APRIL 1944

Chapter One

INTRODUCTION

The process of hand coloring photographs with transparent oils is extremely simple. Generally the first attempt produces a most pleasing and gratifying result.

Black and white prints suffer greatly by comparison to one properly colored in oils. The presence of color alone affords us greater enjoyment and pleasure than the general monochrome rendition. No picture is complete without color. It is nature's beauty mark and actually demanded in pictorial compositions for a true, lifelike, natural effect. A photograph well done in transparent oils will convey a far greater artistic and realistic impression than that obtained in black and white photography.

In this comprehensive treatise on photo coloring an attempt has been made to thoroughly cover every conceivable angle and problem that may present itself in this color process. Wherever possible the procedure and technique has been simplified without sacrificing the ultimate result. It is true a certain appreciation and knowledge of color harmony is beneficial. However, the lack of this should not discourage the amateur. Certain fundamental principles may appear to be elementary statements but they are set down in almost repetitious form in order to establish them in the mind of the reader. When these few basic fundamentals are absorbed, it is possible for anyone to create colorful photographic masterpieces.

This complete treatise on the art of photo coloring will serve as a textbook and reference guide for the amateur and professional colorist alike. It will be especially helpful to the amateur who is accustomed to black and white photographic values, gradations and tonal moods and will prevent him from becoming color conscious when working in transparent photo oils. The tendency towards overcoloring and undercoloring is largely eliminated. The extremely simplified and concise procedure, herewith outlined, along with the color formulas and harmony combinations, will inspire the beginner towards the creation of true, realistic and artistic color impressions.

In most cases a good example of hand coloring in photo oils is far superior to natural color photography itself and certainly much easier and less expensive in rendering the final result. Photo oil coloring also has another definite advantage inasmuch as it can be controlled to the extent where the tone values and pictorial composition can be changed or altered to suit the individual taste.

In order to fully appreciate the unlimited possibilities of this new medium, the intelligent application of photo colors is necessary. Here is a simple controlled color process that will impart extra realism to any picture and provide one of the most fascinating and enjoyable phases in connection with photography.

Chapter Two

COLOR HARMONY

Color is one of nature's most important gifts to mankind. It surrounds us constantly and unfortunately is, more or less, taken for granted by the average person. Yet, it alone is primarily responsible for the innumerable impressions we term as beautiful. A greater appreciation and understanding of this magic, known as color, will prove of infinite benefit to those working with it and afford greater enjoyment out of life in general.

The fundamental principles pertaining to the use of color and basic laws governing color harmony should be thoroughly studied and familiarized by the beginner before any attempt is made to actually color a photograph in oils. No attempt has been made to enter into a highly technical treatise on the numerous phases of color harmony and mixture of pigments. The following concise, simple, basic color facts as set forth, however, will provide the student with the color knowledge necessary for the successful and artistic application of colors.

There are many systems of color study. Some are based on three colors. Others on six, and still others using eight and twelve colors. The fact still remains, however, that the three colors,—Red, Yellow and Blue will yield any required color and yet they cannot be produced by the mixing of any other pigments. For this reason Red, Yellow and Blue are called pure or Primary colors.

The mixture of any two Primary colors creates a new color known as a Secondary. The Primaries Red and Yellow produce the Secondary color, Orange; Yellow and

Blue make Green; and Blue mixed with Red yields the Secondary, Violet.

The intermixture of a Primary color and its nearest Secondary color produces another step in the color cycle known as an Intermediate. Thus, the Primary Yellow and the Secondary color, Orange, when mixed together produce the Intermediate color, Yellow-Orange. The mixture of Yellow and Green yields a Yellow-Green. The Intermediate colors produced by mixing with their nearest Secondaries are: Yellow-Orange, Red-Orange, Red-Violet, Blue-Violet, Blue-Green and Yellow-Green.

The Photo Oil Color Chart on Page 10 shows the Primary, Secondary and Intermediate colors and the combinations used in their mixture.

COMPLEMENTARY COLORS. When two colors are mixed together in equal quantities and produce a neutral gray they are called complementary colors and are in harmony with one another.

By mixing a Secondary color with the Primary not used in its mixture we produce a neutral gray. For example, Green is the Secondary obtained by the mixture of Yellow and Blue, leaving Red as the only remaining Primary color. Red, therefore, is the complement of Green and when the two are mixed together, produce a neutral gray. The same is true of Orange, which is the Secondary produced by the two Primaries, Yellow and Red. Blue, the remaining Primary not used in creating Orange, is called the complement of Orange. The two when mixed together in equal quantities yield a neutral gray and are known as Complementary Colors.

The colors in the Photo Oil Color Chart are so arranged that the Complementary colors are opposite each other. Yellow, for example, is opposite its complementary, Violet; Red is opposite its complement, Green; Blue opposite its complement, Orange; Yellow-Orange opposite Blue-Violet; Red-Orange opposite Blue-Green and Red-Violet is opposite its complement, Yellow-Green.

We have learned that by mixing a given color with its

COLOR CHARTS

* ★ Photo Oil Color Chart
* ★ Color Harmony Chart
* ★ Black and White to
       Color Example
* ★ Applicator Preparation
* ★ Color Application

PHOTO OIL COLOR CHART

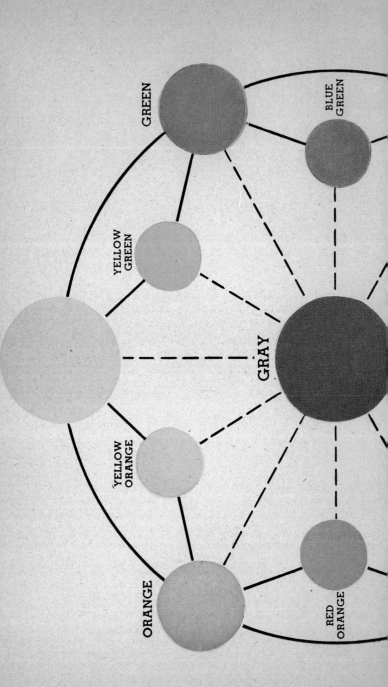

YELLOW

GREEN

YELLOW GREEN

BLUE GREEN

GRAY

YELLOW ORANGE

ORANGE

RED ORANGE

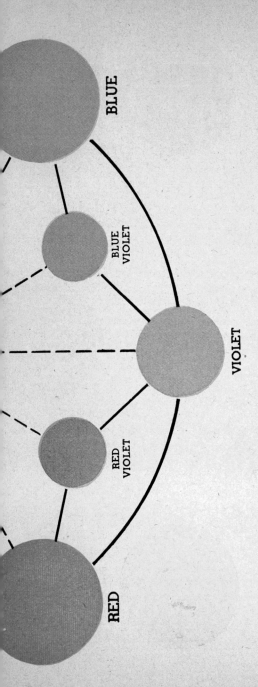

The above color chart has been prepared with standard transparent photo oil colors represented as follows:

PRIMARY COLORS

Yellow —Cadmium Yellow
Red —Carmine
Blue —Utramarine Blue

SECONDARY COLORS

Orange —Cadmium Orange
Violet —Cobalt Violet
Green —Medium Green

INTERMEDIATE COLORS

Yellow Orange —Cadmium Yellow Deep
Red Orange —Cheek
Red Violet —{ 1 part Cobalt Violet
{ 1 part Carmine
Blue Violet —{ 1 part Ultramarine Blue
{ 1 part Cobalt Violet
Blue Green —Viridian
Yellow Green —Oxide Green

COLOR HARMONY CHART

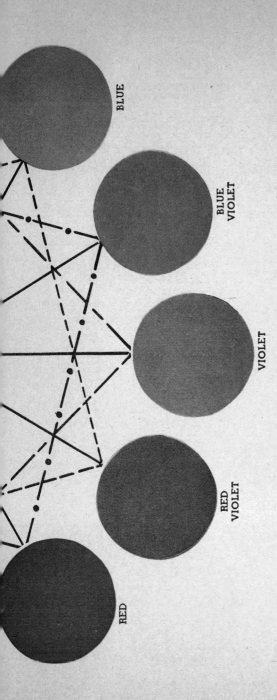

RED

RED VIOLET

VIOLET

BLUE VIOLET

BLUE

The Primary, Secondary and Intermediate colors of the Photo Oil Color Chart are here arranged so as to form a complete circle. This arrangement simplifies the method of compiling innumerable Complementary, Triadic and Analogous color harmony combinations. Each color is directly opposite its complement, the combination of which produces neutral gray. The colors here reproduced are represented by the same photo oil colors used in the Photo Oil Color Chart.

W. J. Seemann

Mission San Juan Capistrano

Black and white study used in the step by step
coloring procedure described in Chapter Four.

W. J. Seemann

Mission San Juan Capistrano

Colored with transparent photo oils. Note the
improvement over the black and white original.

Preparing The Cotton Pointed Skewer

A piece of long fibre cotton is held in place between the thumb and index finger of the left hand.

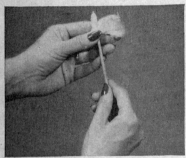

Fold the cotton over and twist the skewer with the right hand and roll into a tight wad.

Cotton will adhere better to the skewer if the end is slightly dampened before twisting the cotton into place.

Using The Cotton Tuft

First the wadded cotton is dipped lightly into the desired oil color.

By lightly rubbing it on a piece of paper, the color is evenly distributed on the working surface of the cotton tuft.

After testing on the working paper, the color is then smoothly blended into the desired area of the photograph.

complement, both colors are neutralized and produce a neutral gray. This is a very important fact to keep in mind as it will greatly aid the artist in achieving the proper tonal quality of the scene to be colored. If a picture calls for a sombre key, such as a fog or dreary rain scene, the artist should use mostly neutralized, or grayed colors. If, however, a picture calls for colors in a high key, where tones should be clear and transparent, a proper understanding of complementary colors will help the colorist to avoid inappropriate gray or muddy mixtures.

The colors shown on the Photo Oil Color Chart, page 10, are as bright as they can be created with transparent photo oil pigments applied to regular white photographic paper and rubbed down to an even smooth tone. Tints are lighter tones of these colors and are produced by adding white or a transparent dilutent. Tints of Blue, Red and Yellow are Baby Blue, Pink and Pale Yellow. Any color that is darker than those on the Color Chart is called a shade of that color. For example, Black added to Red yields the shade, Maroon. Black added to Green produces the shade, Olive Green. Another method used to darken or produce a deeper shade of a color, is to use its complementary color. To deepen Blue, add Orange; to get a darker shade of Red, add green.

White, Gray and Black are natural tones in which no color is visible. White mixed with a color dilutes the intensity of the color and produces a tint but it does not brighten the color. Yellow is the brightest color produced by pigments and is known for its intense and advancing character.

Harmonious complementary color combinations may be obtained with colors full strength or paled to produce soft delicate tints. Likewise, darkened shades of complementary colors are in harmony. Although complementary colors can be depended upon to produce harmony care must be taken in their selection and relation to the entire picture. They should seldom be used in full intensity unless balanced with White, Gray, Black or other neutral-

izing combinations. Large areas of complementary colors
should be avoided whenever possible unless their brilliance
is substantially minimized and toned down. Even in vivid
sunset scenes, where these extreme combinations are apt
to appear, the colors must be brought into harmony by
subduing one or both to prevent an overpainted and harsh
impression. Broadly speaking, when used in full intensity,
complementaries should be confined to extremely small
areas as accents to enhance the color mood. The tonal value
of each color should be equalized with a careful consideration of its complement in relation to the color balance
of the composition.

On Page 12 the Primary, Secondary and Intermediate
colors of the Photo Oil Colar Chart have been arranged so
as to form a complete circle. Each is in its proper place in
relation to the other colors of the chart. This arrangement
simplifies the method of arriving at various harmony combinations and is known as a Color Harmony Chart.

In compiling both the Photo Oil Color Chart and Color
Harmony Chart, we have used actual reproductions of
standard transparent photo oil pigments as they appear
when rubbed down on white photographic paper. Hence,
the artist can instantly make up any of the numerous harmony combinations without the inconvenience of trying
to compare and match color samples with colors foreign
to photographic work. If the artist does not possess certain
specified colors, substitutions can be made from the list
of similar and related colors listed in the Photo Oil Color
Guide, page 133.

TRIADIC HARMONY: A color equidistant between two
complementary colors forms a three color combination
known as Triadic harmony. By using the line joining two
complementary colors, as the base of a triangle, the apex
of the triangle so formed will point to the third harmonizing color. Thus, on the Color Harmony Chart we find
the line connecting Red, with its complementary color
Green, represents the base of the triangle and the apex
points to Yellow-Orange. Therefore, Red, Green and Yel-

low-Orange form a three color combination known as Triadic harmony. Again, using Red and Green as the base and forming our triangle on the opposite side of the base line, we find the apex rests on Blue-Violet as the third color. Hence, Red, Green and Blue-Violet are also in Triadic harmony. By forming similar triangles from the various dotted lines, adjoining the colors of the Color Harmony Chart, we find such Triadic harmonies as Red-Violet, Yellow-Green and Blue; Yellow-Orange, Blue Violet and Red; Yellow, Violet and Blue-Green; Orange, Blue and Yellow-Green; and many other combinations (See page 12).

A combination of two Triadic harmonies, using the same triangle base, produces a new combination of four colors made up of two pairs of complements and known as double Triadic harmonies. For example, in using the line connecting Red and Green as our triangle base, we find that the apex selects Yellow-Orange as our third color. By utilizing the same base and forming our triangle on the opposite side we acquire Blue-Violet as the third color of our second Triadic harmony. Therefore, the combined colors, Red, Green, Yellow-Orange and Blue form a four color combination of double Triadic harmonies. Their arrangement on the Color Harmony Chart is such that they form a square, the corners of which point to each color. By forming similar squares based on other colors of the chart, many diversified harmony combinations can be created.

Double Triadic harmonies, such as this, are naturally composed of strong contrasty, complementary colors and should be used with utmost discretion. Otherwise, an over-painted, gaudy and exaggerated effect may be the result. This type of bold harmony, if used judiciously, has its advantages in such scenes as sunsets where contrast values are demanded for a true color impression.

ANALOGOUS COLOR HARMONY. When colors which are adjacent to each other on the Color Harmony Chart are used in combination, they are said to be in analogical harmony. Simple analogous color combinations are Yellow and Yellow-Orange; Blue and Blue-Green; Blue and Blue-Violet, etc. Analogous color groups of three colors are made up by selecting a color and using the neighboring color on each side of it. As an example, take Red, its two neighboring colors are Red-Orange and Red-Violet, thus completing the combination. Other three color Analogous harmony groups are Green, Blue-Green and Yellow-Green; Yellow-Green, Green, and Yellow; Orange, Red-Orange and Yellow-Orange; etc.

A complete and comprehensive list of harmonious color combinations could be listed but the author feels these would confuse rather than be helpful to the beginner. It is of utmost importance, however, that the student study the colors which surround us in everyday life. Nature has supplied us with an unlimited number of harmonious color combinations.

Observe Nature's color chart and try to visualize which pigments, or mixture of pigments, will represent the color seen. Study an evening sunset and watch the gradual change of the soft delicate colors. Watch for the harmonious color combinations in flowers, birds, forests, mountains, oceans, lakes and every other form of Nature's color scheme. Note the countless color combinations, the restricted use of bright and vivid colors in relation to the overall mass of subdued and neutralized tints and shades.

Such analysis and study of Nature's colors will help the artist tremendously in rendering the coloring of photographs in a natural and realistic manner. Photographs, after all, are only black and white reproductions of Nature's wonders. It remains for the colorist to make the picture complete by the proper selection and application of colors. When accurately applied, color will give a photograph perspective and the feeling of depth and reality seldom obtained in a black and white print.

It is also recommended that the student carefully study good oil paintings, or reproductions, whenever possible. Note how the sky is handled, the restrained and subdued colors used in the distance, and the increasing boldness of these colors as they are applied to the intermediate distance and foreground objects. Note how the proper use of these colors creates a feeling of depth. Look for the many shades and tints used in the shadows, halftones and highlights. Also the effect obtained by bold strokes of broken color carefully applied in the appropriate places.

The bold technique used in opaque oil painting cannot satisfactorily be applied to the coloring of photographs in transparent oils but a modified version of this technique can be employed which will create an artistic masterpiece superior in many cases to photographs taken in natural color.

Photographers who use Kodachrome film have an accurate color record of each scene. Outstanding compositions may be duplicated, enlarged in black and white and tinted by using the original Kodachrome transparency as a color guide. This is an excellent procedure to use for those in position to take advantage of it. Frequently, the black and white print can be altered at the artists disposal and improved in both color and composition so as to render a more pleasing and artistic result than that contained in the original color transparency.

Chapter Three

COLORING THE PHOTOGRAPH

Only certain surfaces of photographic papers are suitable for coloring with transparent photo oils. The regular glossy prints turned out by so many photo finishers are not adaptable to satisfactory photo tinting. Such a surface is too hard and will not absorb sufficient color to register the proper tones. Usually the Matt, Semi-Matt, Velvet and similar dull surfaces are recommended as these grades are soft enough to absorb the full strength of the oil colors and produce excellent results.

The print or enlargement to be colored should be properly printed and developed so as to give clear highlights and good gray details in the shadows. Dense blacks in a photograph are difficult to color as the transparent oils are not heavy enough to register the proper tones.

If enlargements or prints are to be made by commercial photo finishers it should be mentioned that they are to be colored in photo oils. Thus, the finisher can help in the selection of a suitable grade of paper and process the photograph accordingly. A good photographic print is the basic foundation for successful and artistic results.

Coloring with transparent oils differs greatly from actual painting in opaque colors. With opaque pigments the design is built up by the artist through the skillful application of colors to create perspective, depth and the rotundity of objects. The entire picture is built upon a blank piece of canvas. In photo coloring the problem of drawing and sketching has been eliminated as the photographic image forms a complete picture in monochrome.

Transparent oil colors when applied to any area of the photograph, imparts color to that area still allowing the photographic image to register through the transparency of the colors themselves.

Before starting the actual process of coloring it is necessary for the student to obtain a well balanced selection of transparent oil colors. There are several well known reliable concerns which specialize in the manufacture of Photo Oil Colors and offer a most complete selection of colors ground and mixed especially for use on photographs. These may be purchased in most art or photographic stores.

In order to acquaint the beginner with the trade names and similarity of the many standard photo colors available, a comprehensive Photo Oil Color Guide, page 133 has been compiled. The colors listed are standard with the majority of oil pigment manufacturers and are contained in most of the photo oil color sets on the market today. Under each major color is a list of additional oil colors which are so similar in their composition and reproduction that they may, for all practical purposes, be used as a substitute or alternate color.

Each color manufacturer's standards may not be exactly the same and this accounts for the slight variation not only in shade but also strength. Many colors listed under the key color in the Photo Oil Color Guide are an exact match but known by a different trade name. In some cases the variation in tone is practically negligible. In a few instances the difference may be slightly noticeable but the color is so closely related to the listed tone that it can be safely substituted without affecting the final result.

This valuable Color Guide has been produced primarily to familiarize the student with the most common photo oil colors available and to supply him with a reference guide whereby any desired shade may be instantly selected. If the artist does not have at his disposal a recommended color for a certain effect, an appropriate substitute may be selected to create the same result. It will also prove extremely helpful in composing harmonious color combinations with the various transparent photo oils available.

In compiling this guide no attempt has been made to make it complete as its present simplicity and effectiveness would be lost. The colors listed offer a variety far in excess of the quantity required by the average artist. Ordinarily, a well balanced selection of from fifteen to twenty colors will answer the requirements of the most advanced colorist.

The first step prior to the application of colors is the treating or sizing of the photographic surface with Medium. This treatment with Photo Medium will provide a tooth on some photographic papers which have a semi-hard surface permitting the application of heavier and denser colors. On papers of a softer nature, a coating of medium will treat the surface to prevent the absorption of too much color. In either case, this sizing with Medium is essential for an even and smooth application of transparent oils. A light application of Poppy Oil may be used as a substitute for photographic Medium if necessary.

Photographic Medium is available in two forms. One is a jelly-like substance in tube form which must be mixed with turpentine before using. The other is a liquid Medium which requires no mixing whatsoever. Medium is also used as a dilutent to reduce the strength and density of the oil colors.

The surface of a photograph is treated by simply applying a small amount of medium to a wad of cotton and lightly rubbing the surface with an even application. Any surplus Medium should be removed with a piece of clean rag or cotton.

Cotton is the principal "tool" used in photo coloring. Oil colors are applied to the print with cotton tufts or wads and rubbed on and wiped off to secure the desired result. These cotton tufts are made by twisting long fibre cotton into the size desired for the area to be colored. Usually large tufts or wads are made up for the coloring of large areas and smaller tufts for general use.

For fine detail coloring on small areas, cotton may be twisted on the pointed ends of wood skewers, sticks or toothpicks. These are prepared by taking a short piece of cotton between the index finger and thumb of the left hand and twisting it onto the pointed end of the stick held in the right hand. The cotton will adhere better to the wooden sticks if the end is dampened slightly before twisting the cotton into place. Small rough notches cut in the stick or skewer, near the point, will hold the cotton in place and prevent it from slipping off while working. The amount of cotton twisted onto the skewer can be altered to make color applicators of various sizes.

Small artists spotting brushes also come in handy for fine detail work and coloring where strong, heavy tones of an opaque density are demanded.

A small amount of each desired color is squeezed from the tube onto a white plate, glass or palette. Use only very little of each color as transparent oils will go a long ways. A wad of cotton is dipped lightly into the color and gently worked on a piece of white paper to evenly distribute the paint over the working surface of the cotton tuft. Do not rub too hard or most of the color will be transferred onto the working paper before application to the print. Inasmuch as many colors look exactly alike on the pallette, this is an excellent procedure to follow as it gives a color test on paper before actually applying the paint to the photograph. The cotton tipped skewers or toothpicks are, likewise, dipped lightly into the paint which is evenly distributed on the cotton by twisting and rubbing lightly on the working paper. This eliminates the possibility of depositing a large amount of unwanted color on the photograph.

Use enough color so that it will easily cover the area to be tinted. Rubbing lightly with a circular motion will greatly aid in producing a smooth and even colored surface. Should too much color be removed in achieving the desired effect, repeat with a second heavier application directly over the first. If the colored area appears too dark, or needs blending from a darker shade to a lighter tint, then rub with a clean wad of cotton until the right density is secured. By proper rubbing a strong color may be reduced and weakened to almost any desired tint. Actually the pigments are blended onto the surface of the paper exercising care not to remove too much of the color. In case excessive color is wiped off the result will appear flat and lifeless. It is of utmost importance that the tones be laid on in heavy enough applications to impart the feeling of strength and impression of realism.

Do not be alarmed if the color overruns into adjacent areas as it can be rubbed down with clean cotton or entirely removed with turpentine. In the majority of cases when one color is applied directly over another it will obliterate the first color. This, of course, depends on the subject and the colors used. For instance, in tinting a portrait, the flesh color when applied and rubbed down will overlap onto the hair and background of the picture. However, when the hair and background colors are put on they will usually blend into the overlapping flesh color and not be noticeable.

As mentioned before, if it is desirable to remove accidently applied color, the area can be cleaned with turpentine and cotton. The white borders of a finished photograph are cleaned by dipping a cotton pointed skewer in turpentine and gently rubbing off the undesired color. Frequently, a hard outline is formed between the finished colored area and that from which the color has been removed. Gentle rubbing with a piece of clean dry cotton will eliminate this outline.

Each color should be rubbed down and that particular area finished as much as possible before another color is worked on. Generally large surface areas are colored first, medium areas next and small fine details last. This procedure, however, is left entirely up to the individual. Some artists in painting a portrait will color the background first. Others will finish the entire head and bust, leaving the background until last. It is the contention of

those using the later method that a more balanced relation between the subject and background can be secured
and at the same time maintain the proper key with the
rest of the picture.

In landscape painting it is advisable to start with the
sky first, then proceed to the far distance, middle distance
and finally the foreground objects.

A common mistake made by most beginners is that of
rubbing off too much color from the first areas painted.
A large colored area, such as a sky, will appear the right
tint when compared to the grey monotone values of the
adjacent uncolored areas. However, after the rest of the
picture has been colored, the sky will appear too light.
This is attributed to the fact that surrounding colors reduce the intensity and color value of the sky making it
appear lighter than originally intended. In many cases it
is necessary to correct this and apply a deeper color to the
affected area in order to create the proper color balance
with the rest of the picture. The beginner should always
leave the first colored areas slightly darker than desired
and tone down later if necessary.

Highlights are usually the brightest parts of the picture
and are represented on the original print by the whites of
the photographic paper. Shadows are the dense dark portions of an object and will vary from medium grays to
dark blacks. The intermediate tones, halftones and middle
tones are all the same and generally represented by a soft
tonal gradation between the shadows and the highlights.

The ground, base or basic color is the first color undercoating applied all over the object and is representative of
its predominating tone. Highlights, in some cases, may
be interpreted by simply rubbing down or lightening the
base color. Other highlight colors may be reduced in brilliancy by diluting with Medium or mixing with white. In
the following pages where white is mentioned for the highlights, any of the three methods may be employed depending upon the effect to be achieved. Where the highlights
on the original print are gray, white is required to bring
out the desired result. White is also demanded in the mix-

ing of opaque density colors to denote intense and vivid highlights.

Deep, dense shadows are enhanced by the addition of heavy warm or cold color applications, rendered in keeping with the general color balance of the picture. Where the deep shadows on the print are dark grays and blacks, it is often necessary to lay on the paints in almost opaque density to impart a realistic color impression.

Touches of color are faint blendings of one color with another to subdue or intensify the tonal value and brilliancy of the color. Strokes of color may range from soft blendings of definite shades to the heavy bold applications required in broken color technique.

Whenever possible always color by daylight, preferably in a cool north light, unaffected by direct reflections of sunlight. Should it be necessary to work under artificial light, use a blue or "daylight" bulb. The ordinary house lamp produces a decided yellowish light which greatly alters the color value of the paints as they are applied to the photograph. A picture colored under such conditions will have an entirely different appearance by daylight inspection and will not be representative of the coloring as originally intended.

One of the most important items an artist can possess is a scrap book with color reproductions of portraits, landscapes, flowers, animals, still life objects and innumerable other subjects. An extensive reference library may be compiled from magazine illustrations of color photo reproductions. This, along with the artists own color notes made from personal observation, will prove of inestimable value to both beginner and professional colorist alike.

Chapter Four

LANDSCAPE COLORING

There is a trite but true expression which states, "Experience is the best teacher." Realizing the importance of giving the student practical experience in photo coloring, along with a complete knowledge of the methods and descriptive terms used, we are devoting this entire chapter to the thorough analysis and painting of a photograph. The following comprehensive step by step procedure will fully acquaint the amateur with the proper use of the tools involved and the diversified methods employed in achieving the desired effects.

The selection and size of the cotton wads and cotton pointed skewers or toothpicks is left entirely to the discretion of the beginner. Select the size applicator in relation to the area to be colored. Most of the work in this demonstration will be done with cotton pointed skewers as fairly large areas can be covered and rubbed down without excessive over-lapping of colors into adjacent parts of the photograph.

It is mentioned quite frequently in the following pages about colors being blended or mixed with other colors. This does not necessarily mean that the colors are mixed together before applying to the photograph. In many instances an appropriate base, or ground color, is rubbed into a certain area and other colors are applied directly over this. Thus, the two are blended or mixed directly on the photograph. For example, yellow applied over a blue sky will produce a greenish-blue tint. Likewise, warm brown rubbed over a blue-green will yield a dark greenish-brown tone.

Certain standard colors such as Ultramarine, Veridian, Verona Brown, Raw Sienna and others are recommended from time to time. It is not definitely implied that these specific colors be used, in fact, similar colors under various trade names may be satisfactorily substituted. Occasionally a color is mentioned only in a general way, such as light yellow, medium green, dark blue, etc. The exact color selection is left entirely with the artist depending upon the pigments at his disposal and the particular impression he is endeavoring to create. It would be impractical to suggest a Chinese Blue where an Ultramarine or Cobalt Blue would be more appropriate in the composition. Or where a light yellow is recommended, the artist may find that Naples Yellow is ideal for a situation where Cadmium Yellow, Chrome Yellow or Indian Yellow, would be out of place.

By leaving the color selection up to the student, a certain amount of imagination is required on his part which will prove beneficial later on.

Frequently, a scene demands the use of bright, vivid spots of color which ordinarily cannot be applied by the usual rub off method. Intense foreground highlights, brilliant colored flowers and other objects, generally must be rendered in opaque and semi-opaque applications to produce the desired effect. In such instances it is advisable to apply the dense color with a small spotting brush. If handled properly and carefully matched and blended with the rest of the picture, these touches of brilliant color will go a long ways toward the achievement of a truly artistic effect.

Heavy applications of colors, with practically no rubbing down, are very effective in photo coloring. These are particularly adapted to the broad, dense shadows usually encountered in pictures of trees and shrubbery. Here the colors must be laid on quite heavy with very little rubbing, otherwise the full density of the color will be weakened and its effect lost.

Glance at the finished colored photograph of the Mission San Juan Capistrano. Note how the heavy shadows are handled in the distant foliage and the foreground pepper tree. The colors were applied with a cotton pointed skewer and laid on with short dabs, or strokes, following the physical contours of the object. On the pepper tree, in the upper right foreground, bold heavy strokes of blue, blue-green, brown and medium green were used with little or no rubbing or blending required to produce a natural, yet artistic impression. This is a modified version of the broken color technique used so extensively in regular opaque oil painting. The use of these vigorous strokes of heavy paint contribute a much desired contrast in shadows, halftones and highlights, creating a finished result that seems to sparkle and teem with vitality.

It is suggested that the student obtain a photograph, with basically the same elements as those contained in the Mission photograph, to be used for our coloring lesson. By actually applying the colors and combinations, the beginner will marvel at the simplicity of the process and excellent results achieved. This practical experience in coloring will be worth more than thousands of descriptive words.

On pages 14, 15, will be found two photographs of the Mission San Juan Capistrano. One is the original unpainted black and white print and the other is the same picture finished in transparent photo oils. The following description is the step by step procedure used to produce the completed color result.

STEP No. 1: The original photograph has been printed on a dull finish paper and is ready to be treated with a preparation of Medium. The Medium, already prepared according to instructions, is rubbed onto the surface of the print with a swab of cotton. An even coating is obtained by using a circular motion when applying. The print should now be allowed to set for several minutes after which the surplus Medium is wiped off with a clean piece of cotton. The photo is now ready for coloring.

Step No. 2: The sky is the first area to be colored. A tuft of cotton is dipped into a strong blue color such as Ultramarine and rubbed on a piece of paper to equalize the paint on the cotton. The extreme upper part of the sky is now covered with this strong blue and evenly rubbed into the surface of the photograph. Towards the middle of the sky, Chinese Blue is rubbed on and blended into the deep Ultramarine Blue. As the horizon is approached the blue is gradually lightened up to produce a light faint tint. This is accomplished by starting at the horizon with a clean piece of cotton, rubbing down to the right tint and gradually blending into the middle part of the sky. The blue at the horizon is allowed to overlap into the trees and distant mountain.

The same tuft of cotton used in working the blue sky color at the horizon, is lightly dipped into a little Rose Madder or Carmine and blended into the sky at the horizon. This faint tint of red neutralizes the blue of the distant sky and creates the desired haze impression. The three different tints of blue used in coloring the sky; dark blue in the upper part; medium blue in the middle sky; and a light subdued blue at the horizon; greatly emphasizes the feeling of aerial perspective.

The distant mountain is next treated with a light tint of Raw Sienna and merged into the light blue, overlapping sky color. By keeping this color very light and toned down with the faint blue, an excellent haze interpretation is obtained in keeping with the perception of depth. A general tone of Raw Sienna is next laid on the Mission walls and evenly rubbed down as a base tone. This preliminary coloring of the Mission is necessary before the overlapping trees and foliage colors can be inserted.

Step No. 3: The trees and foliage in the middle distance next require our attention. A basic ground color of blue-green, or Veridian, is worked into the shadows and a diluted medium green applied to the highlights. A warm brown, such as Verona Brown, is used for the warm shadows leaving the cool blue-green base color for the deeper areas. These later may be strengthened with additions of dark blue in the coldest parts. Highlights on the foliage are rendered in a light yellow green with the brightest parts intensified with touches of a subdued light yellow or Raw Sienna. A very pleasing effect is created by blending a light warm brown from the warm highlights into adjoining cool shadows, thereby imparting roundness to the foliage. It should be noted that all details and contrast of colors in the middle distance have been slightly subdued in keeping with the effect of atmospheric haze relative to distance. This is particularly noticeable on the top edges of the foliage which are toned down considerably.

The vegetation, seen through the arch on the right, is deliberately kept in a light, neutralized color key, thereby definitely placing it in a plane beyond the mission and creating the necessary depth. The bright vivid flower colors, in the middle distance, are left until the balance of the picture has been completed and then inserted as final touches.

Our attention is next focussed on the immediate foreground objects. The Mission walls should now be finished so that the overlapping tree and shrubbery colors can be added later. Our base color of Raw Sienna has already been applied to the Mission. The earthen walk, under the arches, takes on a decided reddish-brown cast and is best colored with Burnt Sienna. This same color is reflected onto the sides and shady undersides of the arches. The first two arches, in the left foreground, have their shadow areas quite dense and demand a heavier application of Burnt Sienna or Warm Brown.

The remaining two arches, in the center foreground, have their shadows reduced in density by the reflected light cast from the sunlit earthen walk and receive lighter tints of Burnt Sienna as their base color. The deep ceiling shadows, under the arches, are most effective when rendered in a cool contrasting tone. These are first given a tint of a light blue-gray, such as Payne's Gray, and then qualified with touches of blue and violet blended into the deepest parts. Warm tints of Verona Brown and pale Carmine imparted into the shadows next to the highlights, creates a most pleasing effect.

The tree shadows, cast on the outer Mission wall and the shady sides of the arches, respond to the same treatment with variations dependent upon the density of the shadows themselves. The cool shades of blue and violet and the warm tints of Verona Brown and Carmine are stronger in the denser parts and lightened up for the medium shadows. When working in these various different color tones it is essential that they be smoothly and evenly blended into adjacent colors, otherwise an unnatural impression may be created.

The tile roof and exposed bricks, in the broken plaster of the walls, are appropriately colored with Burnt Sienna mixed with a little red. The shadows between the bricks are touches of Sepia, or a cool brown, and intensified with strokes of a dark blue-gray and violet. Highlights on the bricks are brought out in light tints of red. Incidental highlights in the arch shadows are denoted with subdued tints of Raw Sienna. The Mission is now colored far enough along to permit the insertion of the foreground foliage tones.

STEP No. 4: The same colors required to interpret the middle distant foliage are used for the foreground shrubbery but are stronger in color value and contrast. Our cool base tone of blue-green is first applied to all the shadows of the remaining uncolored foliage. The middle tones and highlights are worked in with a medium green and then the highlights rubbed down to a lighter tint. A warm brown, Verona Brown, is next laid in the middle tones and blended towards both the highlights and deep shadows of blue-green.

When applying these colors to the pepper tree, in the upper right foreground, use long vertical strokes following the characteristic swing of the drooping leaves and branches. Small light strokes of pale Carmine are next applied to represent the clusters of small red peppers. These short downward strokes of bright color are best put on with a small brush charged with a minimum amount of paint and brushed on lightly. The foliage highlights are emphasized with a light yellow green and occasional touches of pale yellow and white. Incidental spots of warm brown laid next to the highlights greatly enhances the effect. Shadows cast on the Mission wall and arches by the shrubbery, are quite effective when colored in a cool blue or violet and blended into the base color of Raw Sienna.

Raw Umber is used as a general ground color for the dirt pathway and flower beds. This is rubbed down to almost a neutral gray as the path recedes into the middle distance. The rocks bordering the paths are colored with a neutral gray and their highlights touched up with Raw Sienna and white. The shadows of the rocks take on a dark brown shade mixed with blue. The intense highlights on the rocks are brought out with touches of opaque white subdued with a tint of Raw Sienna or light yellow. These extreme highlights are almost opaque in density and must be heavy in their application to produce the required foreground contrast. As the rocks recede towards the middle distance, the color contrast is considerably reduced and modified. Care must be taken to blend the opaque color, at the top of the rocks, into the neutral gray transparent base tint. When properly done, highlights so rendered, will enliven and vivify the entire picture.

Tree shadows cast on the pathway are worked in a medium cool blue and blended into the original Umber base color. Incidental strokes of Burnt and Raw Sienna give a warm touch to the sunlit parts of the pathway. These same colors are used in finishing up the ploughed earth in the center flower bed.

The foreground flowers, with their profuse display of vivid colors, are applied in almost opaque density with the aid of a small spotting brush. All the flowers are painted in their natural colors in heavy pigments carefully mixed to the right shades before application to the print. The middle distant flowers are handled in a like manner, but the tones are subdued in brilliance in keeping with the interpretation of depth. The extreme "hot" highlights on the Mission walls are likewise applied using opaque white and light yellow. All touches of heavy opaque colors are left until the very last thereby eliminating the possibility of smearing into other parts of the picture.

The photograph is now complete except possibly for a slight alteration of color here and there to intensify or reduce the contrast of an object or area, thus improving the color balance of the entire study. The color which has overlapped onto the white border of the print is removed with a cotton pointed skewer and turpentine. The finished colored photograph should now be placed away in a dustless spot to thoroughly dry out before varnishing, mounting and framing.

Chapter Five

FACTS ON LANDSCAPE COLORING

ATMOSPHERIC HAZE. The presence of atmospheric haze and its true interpretation in color is one of the most important steps in successful photo coloring. Its correct rendition will produce a perception of depth and aerial perspective seldom obtained in uncolored photographs.

It is a known fact, and one the artist should always remember, that the atmospheric haze, separating the foreground, middle distant and far distant objects modifies the colors, details and contrast of those objects. The greater the intervening distance the more subdued and diminished these elements become. A mountain in the remote distance, for example, we know is spotted with trees, rocks and vegetation almost identically the same in color value as similar foreground objects. Yet, in coloring the mountain, light indefinite shades and tints of brown and green are greatly subdued by the blue and violet tones representative of the atmospheric haze.

Foreground objects are generally depicted in heavy colors with strong contrasts between light and shade with details well worked. As objects recede into the middle distance, the colors are neutralized considerably with details and contrasts slightly diminished. The far distant background is rendered in almost flat, weak tints predominated by the haze colors, blue and violet. All details and contrasts are now reduced to an absolute minimum, being practically indistinguishable. This important principle of diminishing details, contrasts and subdued color values, creates the realistic impression of depth and perspective so vital for the successful portrayal of all landscape scenes.

COLOR BALANCE AND COMPOSITION. The composition of any picture should be so planned that there is one major center of interest. Around this everything else is subordinated or built up to strengthen the effect of the main feature, thereby producing a pleasing arrangement with satisfaction of unity to the eye. In black and white photographs we have composition consisting of the balance between masses, lines, tones, gradations and accents. On the other hand, composition in color pictures is acquired principally through the contrast of colors rather than light and shade.

An excellent black and white composition must be co-ordinated with the proper balancing of colors, otherwise the entire scene will be thrown out of tune. Ordinarily, great care must be used in the application of color to avoid any alteration of balance in the original composition. In many cases the appropriate selection and application of colors will substantially improve a black and white print which lacks good composition. By the use of color, certain masses and tonal qualities may be subdued or accentuated to create a more pleasing relation between the component elements of the pictorial composition. Frequently, with the aid of opaque applications, undesirable objects may be eliminated entirely, thereby greatly improving the general effect.

Color balance is of utmost importance in photo coloring. A bright colored foreground demands a reasonably bright colored background. Likewise, a dull subdued foreground should have a corresponding subdued background. An even scale of color values must be retained.

The color key or theme of the study will materially influence the selection of colors required to maintain a relative balance. Should a scene call for strong, vivid, contrasting tones the same related colors must be carried throughout the entire picture. Moreover, if a photo demands the use of dull, sombre colors to interpret a natural effect, one should adhere to like shades throughout the study for the proper color balance.

This does not mean necessarily that vigorous, bright, high key colors should be entirely eliminated from a composition with a low key color theme. If required and properly inserted, occasional touches of vivid color will enhance the effect and produce a most pleasing result. Such applications must be held to an absolute minimum and used with discretion. Otherwise, the entire picture will be thrown out of color balance.

The colors generally used for distant landscape objects are subdued and neutralized tints of the foreground tones. An analysis of a desert scene in direct sunlight reveals the foreground rocks, hills and other subject matter, rendered in strong contrasty colors. The distant objects, being of similar material composition and governed by like surrounding elements, take on the same coloring used in the foreground objects but being effected by the intervening haze are subdued in color value and contrast. Such a scene usually calls for fairly brilliant colors throughout and altered only slightly to interpret the necessary perspective.

Take as another illustration, a marine or seascape study on a dull, overcast or foggy day. Here the foreground objects are denoted in dull, grayed colors with low contrast between light and shade. This contrast is still further reduced as the scene projects into the background where the far distant objects are practically obscure. Mere suggestions of masses devoid of all detail.

These two extreme examples are pointed out to the student in order to impress upon him the vital importance of always maintaining a related contrast and color balance between all objects in the composition.

LIGHTING CONDITIONS. Another factor which greatly influences the selection and rendition of colors is the time of day depicted and the particular type of lighting dominating the entire picture. An early morning light usually is affected by a pronounced haze and is best interpreted by soft delicate tints and contrasts subdued with blue-

grays and violet-pinks. Highlights cast by the early morning sunlight are of a reddish-orange nature. Midday scenes
take on the full glare of the bright sunshine with colors
rendered in full intensity and contrasts moderately pronounced. As the sun sinks lower in the afternoon sky, a
noticeable reddish hue is imparted to all sunlit objects and
contrasts are greatly increased.

If the light strikes the scene from over the artist's shoulder, full color effects are registered in all objects. When
the predominating light comes from the side, shadows
will increase in density and greater contrast between light
and shade will be noted. Backlighted scenes, where the sun
or light is directly in front of the artist, produce exceptionally strong contrasts with colors leaning towards the
warm browns, oranges, reds and yellows of the late afternoon sunlight.

At sunset the contrasts throughout the picture are increased to the extreme with colors becoming stronger and,
in most cases, more vivid. An interesting change in the
interpretation of perspective takes place in many sunset
pictures, whereby the far distant or middle foreground
objects become our center of interest and the immediate
foreground is secondary in importance. This is particularly
noticeable in sunset scenes which contain cloud effects.
The clouds in the middle distance or near the horizon are
usually brighter in color rendition and stronger in contrast owing to their close proximity to the setting sun. The
foreground objects, being farther away from the light
source, have their coloring substantially toned down and
contrasts diminished.

Foreground objects, such as trees, may appear almost
in silhouette with colors reduced to an absolute minimum.
Under these conditions, depth and perspective is created by
a subdued foreground, a reasonably bright middle foreground and a strong vivid background. Or the perception
of depth may be conveyed by keeping both the immediate
foreground and far distance subordinated to a brilliant
colored middle foreground. In either case, if properly
done, a true sense of reality will be imparted to the picture.

Broken Color. Frequently, we must resort to extremes in contrast rather than actual representatoin to bring out the desired color impression. When certain colors are mixed together they produce a flat, lifeless and most uninteresting mixture. These same colors applied to a picture, separately, in short single strokes and in close relation to one another, create a stimulating vibration of color that actually makes the tone live.

The technique of using broken color, as it applies to regular oil painting, is not wholly adapted to the medium of transparent photo oils. However, a modified version, by which pronounced colors are laid on the photograph, one beside the other, will snap up the effect tremendously. Broken color is effective in the interpretation of intense highlights where heavier applications of paint are permissible. Suggestions of broken color may be used throughout the picture if the colors are carefully inserted and blended so as to maintain the necessary transparency of the pigments. If colors are used in opaque density they must be confined to extremely small areas, otherwise they will over-balance the transparent areas and result in an unnatural effect.

For example, if one is tinting a distant mountain in a desert scene, we cannot mix raw sienna, umber, purple and blue together without obtaining a lifeless, gray mixture. But by using raw sienna as a base color and modifying it with alternate touches of brown, violet and blue, mixed with white and softly blended, we simulate the vibration of atmosphere which makes the colors live.

An ocean scene at sunset responds to the same treatment and has its pictorial effectivneess enhanced by the addition of broken colors. Deliberate strokes of yellow, orange and red, worked with white are used to interpret the sun's reflection across the blue-green water. Such a scene calls for strong contrasts. In fact, the colors used to depict the intense spots of reflected sunlight on the water, are complementary colors of the ocean tones themselves. However, if these were mixed together, only a flat, cold representation would be obtained. But by breaking each color up and mixing with white, a vibrant and stimulating color impression is created.

It is suggested that the student make a preliminary study of the black and white photograph before the actual coloring process is attempted. Visualize the color theme to be used, composition and balance of colors, light conditions under which the picture was taken, the effect of the atmospheric haze and its influence over the colors in bringing out the feeling of depth. Such a predetermined analysis will prove of great benefit in the intelligent and pleasing rendition of a colored photograph.

Chapter Six

SKIES AND CLOUDS

As a rule, the sky is the first area colored in a landscape study, and obviously should receive our attention first. The sky should convey the idea of infinite distance and possess the feeling of aerial transparency. To accomplish this, a translucent color must be used and toned down with parts of various other colors according to the effect desired by the artist.

The color used on the sky, more or less dictates the type of colors to be used throughout the balance of the picture. They will tell us whether it is a bright, sunny day, cloudy or dull, early morning, midday, late afternoon or evening. This close relation of the sky to other objects in the scene is a factor the colorist should always keep in mind.

The sky on a clear day is generally a strong blue directly overhead and graded down to a lighter indefinite blue as it nears the distant horizon. Such a sky is first colored with a strong ultra blue at its zenith. This is gradually blended into a medium blue at the middle distance and softly rubbed down to a light indistinct blue at the horizon. A faint trace of raw sienna or rose madder is lightly blended into the pale blue at the horizon, thereby slightly neutralizing the color and producing the desired effect of aerial perspective. Careful and smooth blending between the deep blue overhead, to the soft gray neutralized blue at the distant horizon is essential to attain a transparent quality of the sky and impression of depth.

At sunrise, or early dawn, the sky colors are frequently modified by the abundance of atmospheric haze. This type of sky picks up suppressed tints of pink-violets, pale yellows and light subdued greens. These colors usually predominate in the average early morning sky and, in many cases, the same combinations will be noticeable in sunset scenes.

Skies in snow studies are seldom rendered in the strong blues so common in regular landscapes. Grayed, neutralized tints are more appropriate in snow compositions as they are in tune with the general cold color theme of the entire picture. The overhead sky is given a moderate blue application subdued with a little rose madder. This produces a cool blueish-gray tint ideal for snow scenes. Near the middle of the sky ,a touch of raw sienna is added to the light blue for a greenish-blue tint. This is gradually blended down into a pale light gray at the horizon. By keeping the colors on the cool side and toned down to weak tints, an even color balance will be maintained.

Sunsets in a cloudless sky require a smooth even blending of several contrasting colors. First, a vigorous blue is imparted to the extreme upper part of the sky and almost instantly merged into a greenish-blue or Chinese blue. A pale tint of vermillion is laid on the sky towards the lower middle and lightly blended into the upper blue and a pale yellow at the horizon.

The success of achieving realism in any sunset scene lies in the proper selection of colors and the care used in their delicate blending. To secure a natural translucent sky effect, clean cotton wads should be used in rubbing down and fusing the contrasting colors. This enables one to keep the colors clear and radiant and still maintain a soft pastel relation between the delicate tints.

Sunsets change rapidly and offer the student unlimited color combinations. Here again, the importance of studying nature's colors is called to the beginners attention. Whenever possible, observe an evening sunset and make notes of the numerous color combinations and their transitions as the sun gradually sinks behind the horizon. One will be surprised and marvel at the innumerable color harmonies presented at sunset.

CLOUDS. Large expanses of sky are greatly enhanced by the appearance of clouds in the composition. Clouds are of many diversified types, shapes, formations and colors. In some pictures they are insignificant in their importance while in others they represent one of the most conspicuous elements of a composition. Clouds have unlimited and changeable color possibilities. The transition of their colors and lighting effects are as varied and rapid as the changing of their formations.

In direct sunlight, clouds consist of cold highlights, warm intermediate tones and cool shadows all delicately blended together. First a basic warm tint of raw sienna is applied and well rubbed down or mixed with white. The highlights are rendered in white softened with touches of pale yellow or blue. On the upper part of the cloud, the intermediate tones are warmed up with a speck of vermillion. As this tint extends into the lower part of the cloud area, it is softly blended through a cool violet into a blue-gray or neutral gray on the far underneath side.

The rotundity of the cloud depends upon the careful blending of shadows, middle tones and highlights. There should be no sharp demarcation of color to render the realistic feeling of buoyancy. The various delicate tints and shades should actually melt, one into the other.

On dull, overcast days, the clouds take on more of the cooler gray tones predominately governed by the light and dark blending of neutral grays in both highlights and shadows. A light tint of neutral gray, warmed up slightly with pale yellow, vermillion and white, is used for the subdued highlights. The middle tones are interpreted with a darker gray qualified with raw sienna and vermillion. The dark underside shadows call for a deep bluish-gray with touches of diluted violet.

As a rule, neutral tint or gray is the basic color used and is altered slightly by the addition of other colors to impart warm or cold tones as required. Neutral tint, with the addition of a little blue and rose madder, or vermillion, produces a soft, pearly gray ideal for use in practically all cloud formations.

Clouds at sunset invariably contribute to a prolific display of brilliant and luxuriant color combinations in vivid contrasts and perfect harmony. The variety of color combinations, cloud formations and types of sunsets are unlimited, yet one will seldom find two alike. There are several methods that can be employed by the student to determine what combinations of colors to use in a sunset scene. The first is by adhering strictly to the harmony of contrasts; the second, by resorting to analogous or associated colors. Both of these will yield pleasing results.

Double triadic harmonies, consisting of four colors are adaptable to sunset scenes which are to be interpreted in contrasting colors. By the use of the Color Harmony Chart on Page 12 several different combinations can be selected. For example, Yellow, being one of the most prominent colors in an evening sunset, is selected as the base color of our harmony combination. We next pick Violet, which is the complement of Yellow. By using the line adjoining Yellow and Violet, as the base of a triangle, we find the apex points to Red-Orange on one side and Blue-Green on the other. Therefore, Yellow, Violet, Red-Orange and Blue-Green are the colors selected for our four color harmony combination.

The visible parts of the sky between the clouds are first colored in the usual manner with soft gradations from a blue-violet, in the upper parts, to yellow-orange at the horizon. The far distant cloud formations, being nearest to the setting sun, are more contrasty and consequently receive brighter renditions than those in the immediate foreground sky. The highlights on the distant clouds are tinted in bright yellow, toned down slightly with white and vermillion. The shadows are colored in a dark violet and blended through a brownish-green into the middle

tones of red-orange. The foreground clouds receive subdued shades and tints of the same colors.

The Color Harmony Chart will prove useful in assem-
bling other four color harmonies. Suppose we take Orange
as our basic color. Blue is its complement with Yellow-
Green and Red-Violet the remaining colors completing
the group. Likewise, with Green as the basis of our combination, we select Red, Yellow-Orange and Blue-Violet to
complete the color harmony. Extreme caution should be
used in handling these vigorous, contrasty colors. They
must be held in restraint and subdued with grayed or
neutralized mixtures otherwise a gaudy, over-painted and
unnatural effect will be imparted to the picture.

Another type of sunset, and one quite frequently ob-
served, is that which has as its general theme, tints, shades
and related tones of one dominating color. The method
used in selecting the proper color combinations is based on
the principles of Analogous color harmony previously described. On the Color Harmony Chart we find the Analogous harmony combination of Yellow, Yellow-Green
and Yellow-Orange. Yellow has been selected as our basic
color which, with its two adjacent colors, completes the
harmony combination. If a contrasting color is desired we
can use Violet which is complementary to our base color,
Yellow. Care must be taken to minimize the effect of the
complementary color or the general Analogous color balance will be disturbed.

In applying these colors to the clouds, Yellow is used
for the highlights. The orange tints are projected into the
halftones and the shadows blended into a soft subdued
violet with qualifying touches of yellow-green. To many
people, a photograph painted with analogous or related
tints and shades, will have the appearance of being tinted
in a great variety of different colors, but actually they are
all dominated by one basic tone. Other Analogous color
harmonies recommended for sunset scenes are Violet, Red-
Violet and Blue-Violet with the complement, Yellow. Red,
Red-Orange and Red-Violet with the complement Green.

Orange, Red-Orange and Yellow-Orange with the complement, Blue.

The use of these various color combinations is not necessarily restricted to skies, clouds and sunsets. In fact, all objects in the study should be dominated by the colors of each combination, thereby maintaining a related color balance throughout the picture.

Broadly speaking, sunsets produce a peculiar phenomenon in respect to the fundamentals of the interpretation of distance and perspective. We have been told that in order to impart depth and aerial perspective to a scene, our background and middle distant objects are subdued in color and contrasts diminished. In sunset studies, however, we find the reverse. Clouds nearest the distant horizon and setting sun, are more intense in their coloring and tonal contrasts than those in the immediate foreground. Colors and contrasts, under these lighting conditions, are subdued as the foreground is approached. This reverse perspective of contrasts and color values is an important factor in conveying a realistic impression to sunset scenes.

Many photographers rely upon the use of filters to give general color correction to a photograph. These filters usually hold back the blue of the sky rendering it quite dark on the finished print. Clouds are emphasized and brought out prominently by their contrast with the darkened sky. If the sky is heavily filtered, and extremely darkened, it is difficult to lay on the transparent colors in heavy enough applications to register the proper tones. In such cases, it is necessary to use the strongest colors available, extra strong photo oils or regular opaque pigments diluted to the desired requirements. Whenever possible, dark filtered skies should be avoided as they do not lend themselves to the delicate pastel tints so essential for a natural transparent and artistic effect.

Many photographic landscapes are immensely improved by the insertion of cloud effects. If clouds are desired to strengthen the composition they may be added during the coloring process. First the sky is colored in the usual manner. The cloud design is then made by removing the sky color, with a cotton pointed skewer and turpentine, leaving the natural color of the paper visible. Generally, the photographic paper is too gray and flat to represent a realistic cloud impression, so highlights and shadows are inserted to produce the necessary roundness.

In many instances, the use of opaque white is required to successfully render artificial cloud formations. Here great care must be exercised to keep the opaqueness of the colors reduced to a minimum. Careful mixing of pigments to the exact shade will produce clear and translucent results. The edges of the clouds should be softly blended into the adjacent sky and toned down so as not to appear artificial. By keeping all cloud colors subdued and evenly blended with soft gradations from the highlights through the halftones into the shadows, a light, fluffy, buoyant feeling is created.

When properly done, cloud and sunset studies can be outstanding examples of the photo colorist's art. The amateur is cautioned, however, against the tendency of becoming color conscious and resorting to indiscriminate and exaggerated displays of harsh contrasty colors.

Think before you paint. Visualize mentally the color combinations and balance before applying. Strive for clean, clear, transparent effects. Avoid muddy and dull mixtures from improperly selected paints. Remember a little common sense mixed with the colors will go a long ways towards achieving that feeling of realism every picture merits.

Chapter Seven

WATER SCENES

One of the most common mistakes made by beginners is the tinting of objects, or masses, in one solid color. Frequently, we see a colored photo in which the ocean or lake is rendered in a single tone of blue or blue-green, trees and foliage in one shade of green, rocks in one tint of brown, etc. Pictures so colored invariably have a flat, lifeless appearance and are not true representations of nature's colors.

A most important rule in photo coloring, and one the student should have indelibly impressed upon his mind, is the fact that the colors of any given object or mass are affected by the reflected light cast from surrounding elements. Take, as an example, a body of water such as a lake or ocean. Its coloring is influenced and altered by the colors reflected from the sky, mountains, trees and other adjacent objects. This necessitates the use of many different tints and shades to properly interpret a true, realistic impression. Reflected colors, as a rule, are never as intense as the color of the original object casting the reflection. Their inter-mixture and blending with the colors of the object itself produces a subdued tone, slightly darker in color value.

Water, often referred to as nature's mirror, is undoubtedly affected to a greater extent by reflected colors than any other object appearing in a landscape. When mastered, the few simple principles pertaining to the true interpretation of reflected colors, will do much towards the achievement of an effective and pleasing result.

OCEAN SCENES. Owing to the large expanse of both sky and water in ocean studies, there is an unusually close relationship between the two respecting their color rendition. Under a dull, hazy morning sky, the ocean water will take on darker shades of the reflected sky colors. For example, the sky may be represented by a light blue toned down with pale tints of violet, rose madder and light yellow.

The water is first given a base color of blue-green. Shadows at the bottom of the large swells are intensified with applications of dark blues and browns and occasionally touches of dark violets and greens. The middle tones are rendered with violet, burnt sienna and medium green blended into the original base color of the water. Highlights are emphasized with strokes of light blue, green and pinkish-violet. Rough white water at the crest of the waves is laid on with opaque white and softened with touches of light blue and yellowish rose.

Seascapes, in midday under a cloudless sky, reflect and absorb considerable blue from the sky. An ocean scene under these conditions is given a base tone of a deep blue, such as Ultramarine or Prussian blue. To interpret the feeling of depth and perspective, the distant horizon is toned down and the base color neutralized with faint traces of violet, pale rose and raw sienna. As the highlights and shadows become more distinct in the intermediate distance and foreground, a variety of colors are employed.

Large masses of moving water pick up dark shades of blue, brown, violet and green. These colors are ideal for the shadows of the wave troughs with lighter variations of the same colors blended into the middle tones. The highlights, which are intense reflections of the sky, are depicted in light tints of blue, pale green and touches of diluted rose madder or a pale pink violet. White caps and broken water, at the wave crests, are treated with white toned down by the addition of a little raw sienna, pale yellow or blue.

At sunset, when the sky registers such colors as yellow,

orange, vermillion and violet, the reflections on the water are carried out in modified tones of the same colors. A blue-green, or Viridian, is an excellent base color for the ocean water at sunset. The far and middle distant waves have their shadows worked with neutralized dark blues and grayish-greens. The highlights call for subdued pinks and diluted violet with incidental spots of light yellow.

Massive foreground waves show a great variety of contrasting tones, all influenced by the strong vivid colors seen at sunset. Deep dark blues, greens and purples are applied to the wave shadows and intensified with sepia and black where necessary. Highlights are inserted with the brilliant reflected colors of the sky, namely, light yellow, orange and red-violet and augmented by strokes of pale greens and blues to produce the desired effect. The whites of the rough water are softened or intensified with tints of the highlight colors.

In each of these three examples of ocean coloring, the sky colors have definitely influenced the selection of tones used in the representation of the water. The dominating color masses, in each instance, have been in direct relation to the sky colors and time of day depicted. Incidental tints and shades contributed to the shadows and highlights are qualifying tones used in obtaining a natural and artistic effect. The important point, for the student to remember, is that water is not truly represented by just one or two shades of blue or green, but a combination of many colors, all in relation and harmony with the surrounding elements. These light and dark color variations, when properly applied, will produce a finished result comparable to many marine studies in regular opaque painting.

BEACH SCENES. When viewed from the shore, the ocean at the horizon, is a strong blue-green slightly toned down with Payne's gray or neutralized with vermillion. As the water nears the beach, its shallowness changes the coloring to a light green blended over large areas. Near the shoreline, at the point where the waves break, the water takes on a decided greenish-brown shade, particularly noticeable at the base of the waves.

The crest of the waves, just before they break, call for a tint of greenish-blue well rubbed down and blended into the shadow colors at the base of the wave. If this blending is carefully done an excellent transparent effect is created. The whites of the waves are applied with opaque white subdued with raw sienna, light blue, green and spots of pale carmine or vermillion.

Wet sand along the beach is effective when colored in a dark sepia at the water's edge, blended through a lighter sepa into a raw sienna, representing the dry sand on the upper beach. Shadows on the sand are strengthened with sepia and burnt sienna. Highlights may be denoted in light yellow or diluted raw sienna and white.

Along rugged coastlines, many rocky formations are included in the composition of the photograph. These sea rocks, frequently protrude out into the ocean and offer the colorist an excellent opportunity to bring out their varied rich colorings. A reddish-brown, such as burnt sienna or warm brown, makes a good base color for sea rocks. The shadows acquire a cool dark brown or sepia with a little black. These are also enhanced by touches of blue and violet in the deepest cool areas. Warm shadows have noticeable tints of burnt sienna with blendings of red-orange or crimson. Highlights on the rocks are rubbed down with raw sienna and then given bold strokes of pale yellow, white and diluted carmine to intensify the extreme spots of reflected light.

Where the water level rises and falls, the rocks show definite shades of mud browns and brownish-greens. Glistening highlights, caused by the water as it trickles off the rocks, are represented with small but heavy strokes of pale yellow, blue and white. These intense highlights are very striking when applied with a small brush using the oil colors in almost opaque density.

LAKES AND STREAMS. Like all other large bodies of water, lakes, rivers and streams have their colors affected by those reflected from adjacent objects. Mountain lakes, at high altitudes, should have their coloring dominated by pronounced blues. Generally, these lakes are deep bodies of water nestled among massive granite formations, void of trees and green foliage, except right at the water's edge where small patches of vegetation are visible.

As a rule, a deep cold blue is an appropriate color to accurately represent lakes in high mountain altitudes. However, this is determined and altered according to the sky conditions and time of day. As an illustration, if large massive clouds are overhead, their reflection on the water produces a warm greenish-blue tint which is especially pronounced at the distant shoreline. The various colors used in portraying the far distant mountains, are reflected and blended into the lake colors. Near the shoreline these are toned down and neutralized to impart perspective and depth to the picture.

Lakes and rivers in the lowlands, lend themselves to predominate tints of greenish-brown. These bodies of water are comparatively shallow and, ordinarily, do not pick up the pronounced blues associated with the representation of deep water. Lakes and rivers at lower altitudes are invariably influenced by the preponderance of greens in the general landscape and are adapted to a base color of medium green. Dark shadows are rendered in cool browns and blended with medium and dark greens in keeping with reflected colors along the waters edge. Distant highlights and reflections call for touches of warm brown and yellow-green.

The water in the foreground absorbs and reflects large quantities of the sky colors. If the sky is blue, the water is treated with strokes of light blue intermixed with medium greens and blue-green. Extreme highlights on still, calm water are best denoted with touches of white subdued with light yellow, raw sienna and pale rose or violet, all closely blended to soften the contrast. Small fast running streams containing rapids and large expanses of broken water, are first tinted with white and then toned down with blue, violet and raw sienna in the highlights and green and brown in the shadows.

WATERFALLS. These beautiful cascades of falling water frequently represent one of the main points of interest in the composition, and consequently should be given careful consideration in their coloring. Waterfalls are first given a coating of opaque white and then streaks of blue, violet and medium green applied to the shadows. The density of these shadow colors is increased and intensified at the base of the falls. Highlights, at the upper part of the falls, are tinted with a light yellow and pale rose intermingled with touches of pale blue and white. The highlight tints are determined principally by the reflected colors of the neighboring landscape objects and should be selected accordingly.

The student is advised to make an earnest and systematic study of oil paintings by prominent artists which illustrate the various types of water scenes described in this chapter. Note the effects achieved by the use of reflected colors in both the highlights and shadows and their relation to the balance of the picture. Study the use of broken color, those heavy strokes of vivid and brilliant tones so adaptable and denoting intense highlights and reflections.

Observe the many different shades and tints required to render the natural effect and artistic representation of water. By visualizing objects and masses as a combanation of many related colors, and not just tonal gradations of one color, the student will have accomplished much towards the achievement of natural realism in the coloring of a photograph.

Chapter Eight

MOUNTAINS, HILLS AND ROCKS

Like all other objects of nature, the colorings of mountains, hills and rocks are entirely dependent on several factors; the nature of the vegetation; the strata composition of the rock formations; the time of day depicted; lighting conditions; and the effect of the atmospheric haze relative to the intervening distance.

MOUNTAINS. Regardless of their understood colorings, distant mountains are substantially subdued in color rendition and toned down to a low flat tint of delicate neutralized hues. These indefinite tones, void of details, are required in rendering the true perception of perspective. Mountains in the middle distance are, likewise, moderately affected by an overtone of the same grayed tints.

Under most conditions, the impression of atmospheric haze is best interpreted by the pale blues and violets of nature's true colors. These, when intermixed and blended with the restrained natural tones of the distant objects, neutralize the colors for the desired effect. Some scenes, however, will benefit greatly by the use of warm pale greens and brownish-greens for haze interpretation. This is particularly true of compositions in the flat lighting of midday or under somewhat dull skies. The selection of proper haze tints is dependent, to a great extent, upon the general color theme and maintaining a correct color balance throughout the picture.

Obviously, the farther objects recede into the distance

the greater is their absorption of the intervening haze. And the less pronounced and indistinct become the details and contrast between light and shade. As an illustration, suppose we study a chain of mountains in an average scene. Those in the first range, or intermediate foreground, are colored in a base of medium brown with patches of dull greens denoting vegetation. These colors may be slightly influenced by the haze tint, dependent entirely upon their position or prominence in the composition.

As we drop further into the background, we find the second range depicted in lighter tints of identical colors but with moderate additions of the prevailing haze tones. Likewise, the details become more generalized and indistinct. Again, as we move deeper into the distance, the third mountain range picks up increased quantities of the haze colors and is rendered in flat tints of blues and violet with contrasts materially reduced. Finally, projecting our attention into the remote distance, we find the mountains are so affected by the intermediate haze that their coloring practically merges into the distant sky. All details, contrasts and tones have been infinitely reduced to a low key with only faint, indistinct masses suggestive of the mountain formations. This step by step variation of diminishing values, between each plane in the picture, is a necessary factor in the natural interpretation of depth and perspective.

The time of day and lighting conditions, under which the picture was taken, vastly alters the density of colors and degree of contrast. For instance, mountains at sunset change rapidly in their color composition generally acquiring more of the blue-violet tints always associated with the evening light. Moreover, contrasts are increased, with the glowing highlights taking on brilliant touches of red, orange, and dark yellow. Shadows are fortified by the addition of strong blues and violets qualified with black where required.

The rule of diminishing color values and contrasts is governed principally by an objects' location in the picture

relative to distance and its absorption of the atmospheric
haze tints. Ordinarily, foreground hills or mountains possess prominent displays of browns with greens inserted for
the trees, bushes, grass and other vegetation. The warm
shadows are worked in darker browns and greens with
the cool parts denoted in a blue-green. Highlights may be
colored in light yellow-greens softened with white and raw
sienna.

Middle distant mountains have their color contrasts reduced, with the patches of foliage represented in semi-flat
tones of light medium greens and raw sienna, slightly toned
down with blue and violet. Cliffs, crags and other rocky
formations, devoid of vegetation, call for rich warm
browns, subdued with blue and violet in the shadows and
raw sienna with white in the highlights.

A pleasing effect is produced by tinting the base of the
distant mountains with violet. Additions of carmine are
imparted to the middle parts and blended into a blue at the
top. Certain times of the day, especially early morning and
late afternoon, when the misty haze is quite conspicuous
at the base of the mountain, the effect is enhanced by re-
versing the color procedure. Hence, blue is used near the
base with carmine added at the middle part and softly
blended into a pinkish-violet at the top.

Massive granite peaks absorb large quantities of the blues
and ultra-violets of the high altitude atmosphere and, in
many cases, have their predominating color theme represented by these two haze tints and neutral gray.

Seasons also have their effect on the coloring of mountains, hills and other objects of nature. Spring prescribes
the bright yellow greens; summer, the darker olive and
brownish greens; fall, the rich browns, oranges and yellows of autumn; and winter, the cool drab browns, grays
and blues. Snow scenes are effective when colored with
cold blues, violets, pink and greens to soften the snowy
whites so symbolic of winter studies.

All colors should be co-ordinated with the principal col-
or theme of the picture, keeping the mountain tones held

back with the gray neutralized tints of the haze colors.
The importance of atmospheric haze and its effect on
colors, cannot be overemphasized. A photograph tinted
with due respect to proper rendition of the intervening
haze will create a feeling of depth, perspective and sense
of reality so seldom acquired in black and white prints.

Rocks: Broadly speaking, rocks are composed and built
up around a grayish base color which is altered according to the general color theme and reflection from the
neighboring elements. Large boulders and stones along a
country roadside, or near green fields and meadows, absorb
up around a grayish base color which is altered according to the general color theme and reflection from the
neighboring elements. Large boulders and stones along a
country roadside or near green fields and meadows, absorb
much of the adjacent green coloring of the nearby objects. A neutral gray tint is first applied and the shadows
strengthened with warm greens and browns. Cool shadow
parts are brought out by the addition of blue. The middle
tones take on a slight greenish-gray tint with a touch of
raw sienna. Cold reflected highlights are almost pure
white, tempered with a little blue and gray. Warm highlights are white toned down with raw sienna and a faint
trace of pale green.

Along mountain streams and lakes, rocks range in colors from cold grays to warm browns. As a rule, cool gray
tones are used on rocks in the shade with deep shadows
intensified by additions of a cool sepia and blue. Highlights are white mixed with neutral gray and blue. Warm
brownish rocks have Verona brown as a ground color, with
darker browns and greens in the shadows frequently modified with touches of violet. The middle tones are warmed
up with a reddish-brown and blended into the highlights
of subdued yellows and pale raw sienna.

Rocky formations along the seashore have a pronounced
rich brown appearance and absorb much of the reflected
colorings from the ocean. Either burnt sienna or Verona
brown makes an excellent undercoating for sea rocks. Cold

shadows are worked with brownish-blacks, blue-violet and dark blue-green. Warm shadows and halftones show noticeable tints of green and reddish-brown. Cold reflected highlights, near the water, are rendered in weak bluish-whites. Warm highlights are depicted in yellows and oranges, subdued in brilliance or grayed to the desired tint.

Desert rocks are subjected to the rich tans, browns and red-oranges so symbolic of the dry, barren wastelands. Owing to the vast expanse of sky, so common in most desert photos, the mountains, rocks, plants and other objects are tremendously influenced by the reflected sky color, which generally is blue and pale violet. This accounts for the usual preponderance of blue and violet tints and shades in most desert pictures. These, however, offer a most pleasing contrast with the reddish-browns, oranges and yellows always prominent in landscapes of this nature. Desert rocks can be portrayed in innumerable diversified color moods according to the time of day and prevailing lighting conditions.

Warm browns such as burnt sienna, umber or Verona brown are ideal base colors. Shadows are accentuated with darker browns and shades of blue and violet. Middle tones are heightened with warm tinges of orange and red with incidental blendings of pale green tones. Highlights acquire restrained tints of medium yellow, raw sienna and white. In the late afternoon light, or at sunset, desert colors are greatly increased in brilliance and intensity with contrasts approaching the extreme.

SAND DUNES. Desert sand dunes are handled in much the same manner except that contrasts are slightly increased with more pronounced blue and violet tones visible in the shadows. Raw sienna is an ideal base color for desert sand. Highlights are denoted with definite light yellow tints. Shadows are covered in dark browns with the insertion of strong blues and violets in the coolest parts. The halftones are faint reddish-brown tints and should be evenly blended into the highlights and shadows, thereby creating a natural impression of flowing lines and roundness to the sand dunes. Remember that strong contrasts, vivid colorings, plus the extreme influence of the blue atmospheric haze, are characteristic of desert scenes and should always be kept in mind by the artist when coloring such views.

Frequently, where gray rocks appear in a landscape, the student is tempted to leave these uncolored and let the gray tones of the photographic paper serve the purpose. It will be found that such a procedure leaves an exceptionally flat appearance to the object especially when surrounded by the other colors of the landscape. A more pleasing and desirable roundness is obtained by first applying a neutral gray tint and then blending in appropriate colors to the highlights and shadows.

Intense highlights on rocks, when touched with heavy applications of paint of almost opaque density, seem to snap up and vivify the entire picture. The desired color is mixed on the palette with white to the exact shade to be used and applied to the photograph with a small spotting brush. The color is not rubbed down but gradually blended with a brush, from the opaque density to the transparent base color of the object.

Chapter Nine

TREES AND FIELDS

It is surprising how often we see the colors of trees and foliage misappropriately applied by the beginner. Many colored photographs have the trees erroneously tinted in a flat green tone, rubbed down and left as complete. Basically, all trees, foliage and vegetation contains an abundance of browns and blues intermixed with their natural green shades. Upon close observation, it will be noted that brown is an important color in the true interpretation of all foliage.

Each variety and species of trees have their own dominating color characteristics. The birch is identified by its pale yellowish-green; the oak by its deep bluish-green; and the pine by its dark brownish-green. The eucalyptus is known for its olive green basic color; the pepper for its bright medium green; and the sycamore for its light yellow green. The general color character of trees is altered and changes with the seasons. In the spring, the light yellow-greens are predominate and representative of the new growth. As summer advances, these colors change to the dark olive and brownish-green shades. In the fall, nature runs rampant with the conspicuous, brilliant, autumn tones, yellow, orange, red and rich warm browns. Trees in winter are subjected to the cool drab grays, blues and brownish-greens. By the proper selection of colors, the artist can create an impression of almost any season desired. Contingent, of course, upon the foliage reproduction in the original black and white photo.

Trees lend themselves to the application of two basic ground colors. One, consisting of a warm medium green, is laid on as an under-tone for the warm parts of foliage. The other, a cool blue-green, is used as an undercoating for the cold shadows. Sunlit highlights are charged with a light yellow-green and intensified with touches of bright yellow and white. A rich warm brown, such as Verona brown or burnt sienna, is used in the halftones of the warm shadows and blended with the green base color. The deep cool shadows are accentuated with blue, violet, sepia and black. Cold highlights in the shadows are treated with cool light blue tints of the reflected sky colors.

In the coloring of a photograph, the artist is not com- pelled to resort to the technique of drawing a tree's gen- eral shape with mass and detail construction. These are al- ready recorded on the photograph in monotones of gray, black and white. By applying a wash of a single green tint to the foliage we impart but slight improvement to the original print. The effect suffers greatly by comparison to a study in which variations of several colors are used.

Some trees, like the oak, walnut and maple have their dense masses of foliage best represented with a smooth, even blending of colors from the darkest shadows, through the halftones and on into the highlights. This gradual tran- sition of tones produces a feeling of roundness to the ob- ject not obtained in any other manner. The pepper, wil- low, palm and similar trees require definite strokes of color carefully following the contour and general sweep of the long hanging branches and leaf formations. Still other types of trees, like the eucalyptus and poplar, have their foliage represented by small distinct clusters of color through which frequent patches of sky are visible. By adopting a color technique in keeping with the physical characteristics of the object, a more natural effect is achieved.

Tree trunks are as varied in their coloring as the foliage associated with each specie. Yet, for all practical purposes they can be classified into two groups. One, is the furrowed bark type of the oak, redwood and pine. The other, is the smooth, silvery toned trunk identified with the birch, poplar, eucalyptus, sycamore and others.

The dark heavy barked, tree trunk is colored first with an undercoating of a cool brown such as raw umber or sepia. The shadows are strengthened with touches of blue and black. Warm tones of burnt sienna are given to the warm shadows and intermediate halftones. High lights are rendered in raw sienna paled with white. Burnt sienna and ultramarine blue are excellent colors for the dark parts of the furrowed bark. The cold highlights are worked up with grays and violet modified with white. Spots of sunlight on the tree trunks are colored with yellow and a tint of vermillion and white.

The smooth, soft, silvery gray tree trunks are first given a base coating of neutral gray. Touches of blue and violet will intensify the shadows. The markings of the split, or peeled off, bark are raw siennaa with accents of a cool brown, like sepia. Blendings of pale greens and violet-grays infinitely improve the effect. Highlights are almost pure white, faintly subdued with raw sienna. Small spots of sunlight on the trunk are very effective if blended with various colors, from the extreme white glaring highlight to the blue-violet shadow. This is accomplished by first adding violet to the shadow then toning through crimson to a pale yellow and a final dash of white. This intense highlight effect is best when done in a modified version of broken color technique and is usually applicable only to immediate foreground objects.

At sunset, trees and foliage absorb the reds and oranges of the late afternoon sun. These, when intermixed with the natural green shades, produce a decided brownish-green cast. A preponderance of warm brown tones are used to depict trees at this time of day. The shadows acquire the usual cool blue-violet shades which, likewise, affect all objects at sunset. The halftones call for the warmer dark browns and the highlights reflect the brilliant tints of the sky, usually yellow, yellow-green and orange. If trees are silhouetted against the sunset sky, they are colored dark brown and the shadows strengthened by darker shades of blue, violet and black. The brilliant highlights, cast by the setting sun, are brought out with touches of yellow, orange and vermillion.

Trees, like all other objects of nature, are affected by the rules of diminishing contrasts and colors relative to the influence of the atmospheric haze. As trees, shrubbery and green fields recede into the background, the contrast between light and shade decreases and details become less distinct. Colors are less intense and pick up the blue of the intervening haze. As the blue-violet haze gathers strength with distance, the highlights change to a cool blue and pale blue-green while the shadows become warm with reddish violets and lavenders.

The following simple formula will greatly assist the amateur in determining the proper colors to be used in the tinting of trees, foliage and all other objects in a general landscape: A basic ground color is first applied representing the dominating color. Highlights are lighter tints of the base color and shadows are darker shades of the same. If the highlights are cold they are touched up with pale blues and white. Warm highlights are pale yellows and yellow-greens modified with white. Cold shadows have blue, violet or black added to the base color. Warm shadows are obtained by the addition of warm reddish browns to the original base tone. All colors used must be co-ordinated with the general color theme of the picture in maintaining an even color balance.

FIELDS. A landscape, with fields of grass in its composition, is handled in much the same manner as other types of vegetation. It is a known fact that each blade of grass is composed of pale yellow green highlights and dark bluish-green shadows. It being virtually impossible to color each blade of grass separately, a general color is first applied and broken up with patches of various other colors to create the desire effect.

A yellow green makes an ideal ground color for a grassy field. Patches of grass reflecting the brightest highlights will predominate with light yellows. Other areas in the shade will take on more of the blue green shadow color. Grass in the extreme deep shadows is accentuated with darker shades of blue and, in some cases, touches of a dark warm brown.

Here again, the color theme of the picture greatly determines the selection of colors to represent grassy fields. In some instances, the grass will have an overall tone of brownish-green, with shadows in darker browns and blues, and highlights charged with warm yellows and yellow-greens. Other fields, representing large areas of dried grain or grass, will benefit with a base color of a warm rich brown such as burnt sienna. Shadows are comprised of dark browns and violet. Highlights are raw sienna and yellow paled with white.

The warm brown of fresh tilled soil is secured with a base color of umber and touches of carmine to bring out the deep, damp, richness of the soil. If the sun has dried out the ploughed ground, raw sienna with blendings of burnt sienna and vermillion will give the desired effect. Dirt roads in landscapes are handled much the same as the ploughed fields using colors leaning more towards the raw siennas and subdued yellows with occasional touches of vermillion.

Fields of wild flowers in landscape studies are usually subordinated to the rest of the picture. Although vivid in their general coloring, they are not worked up in the full, rich, brilliant color details as demanded in close-up still life studies. The patches, or clusters, of wild flowers are first colored in their basic dominating tone with light and dark variations used for the highlights and shadows.

Insofar as the landscape composition is concerned, the middle distant foreground should stand out as one of the brightest parts of the picture with colors applied in strong vivid tones. Color contrast and density of the immediate foreground flowers may be reduced or intensified dependent upon the general composition and color balance. As the flower speckled field retires into the background, the colors, contrasts and details are flattened out and subdued with the blue and violet haze tints in keeping with the interpretation of distance and depth.

It is often desirable, and sometimes necessary, to resort to the use of opaque and semi-opaque color applications in rendering the bold, vivid flower tones. The regular rub off method will not always impart the required density and brilliance for true pictorial effectiveness. Great care must be exercised in both the proper mixing and application of these opaque colors, otherwise their heaviness will appear conspicuous in relation to the transparent colors used in the picture. The color is diluted, mixed with white or other colors, to the exact shade required and usually applied to the photograph with a small spotting brush. Generally, these opaque applications are the final touches in completing the study. The judicious insertion of flowers, by this method, will do much to enliven and stimulate the entire composition.

Chapter Ten

SNOW AND MOONLIGHT SCENES

Photographic studies of winter scenes are greatly improved by coloring in oils. So many people are under the impression that the whiteness of the photographic paper is representative of the snow and requires no additional coloring. Such is not the case. These white portions of the picture appear to have a grayish cast until they are qualified with the proper colors to create the true impression of white snow. It is a known fact that snow is white, yet its association with other landscape objects, rivers, mountains, trees, houses, etc., materially influences and alters its color composition.

Snow scenes characteristically suggest coldness and are best interpreted in a color theme dominated by cold colors. In the light of early morning, snow studies are depicted in a low contrast key. The sky is treated with a subdued pinkish-blue tint produced by first applying a light blue and then blending in a rose or diluted carmine.

The distant snow covered mountains are rendered in the same gray neutralized colors as those used for the sky, with contrasts slightly intensified and held to an absolute minimum. In fact the sky colors, used for the distant mountains, are only faintly augmented with blue or violet to represent the shadow tones. Or lightened with white and diluted rose madder to produce the highlight tint. The difference between the distant mountain shadows and highlights, and the actual sky coloring, is very faint, just a tone or two variation from the darkest to the lightest values. Objects in the middle distance have their contrasts increased and take on more violet in the shadows and a trifle more white, yellow and pink in the highlights. The snow in the foreground has its shaded areas covered with a definite cast of light blue and occasional patches of pink and violet. The foreground highlights call for strong applications of white, yellow and pink. To achieve the true impression of early morning, the snow scene colors should be kept in a low contrast key and in close relation with the sky tones. As a rule, a low contrast of neutralized colors is necessary to achieve the effect of coldness in most snow pictures.

An exception to this is noticeable in snow scenes under a bright, vivid sunset sky. Here the cold effect is accomplished by extreme contrast rather than adherence to the use of similar shades and tints. Sunsets in snow studies appear much more vivid and bright by contrast than other types of sunset skies, particularly when soft formations of haze clouds are present. A sky under these conditions takes on a decided light green appearance in the extreme upper part, with incidental patches of light blue between the clouds. As this color is blended towards the horizon, the sky is worked with a red-orange shade finally merging with a bright vermillion at the horizon.

The foreground snow, in such a scene, calls for white highlights with a noticeable yellow and pinkish tint. The shadows are subjected to light tints of blue violet, and gray. The middle distant snow absorbs additional quantities of blue while the far background mountains are colored with indefinite tones of blue-violet. If a lake is visible, the reflections of the sky colors may be appropriately inserted. The general color of the lake is yellow-green at the far distant shoreline with touches of yellow and orange in the highlights. This is blended into a light green at the middle of the lake and on into a decided blue-green in the foreground water. All other objects such as trees, rocks, houses, etc., are painted in their natural colors with their highlights partaking of the radiant sky tones while the shadows are rendered in shades dominated by the cool blues and violets.

Moonlight snow studies have their colors governed entirely by the general color theme of the picture. Usually the snow will be represented by an overall blue cast and the shadows intensified with dark blue and violet. Highlights on the snow are interpreted in tints of pale yellowish whites symbolic of the reflected moonlight.

The most common snow photograph the artist will encounter is that taken during the midday and affected only by the general light conditions of that particular time. The sky is first colored a pale blue, blended down into a greenish-blue towards the middle and on into a light gray at the horizon. Usually a faint touch of vermillion will neutralize the pale greenish-blue tint and render the required soft pearly grey of the distant sky. Objects in the remote distance are colored the same as the sky at the horizon but slightly intensified with more blue and violet. The distant snow is a decided blue and is gradually blended into the white snow of the foreground. The whiteness of the foreground snow is emphasized by faint blendings of blue, violet and pinkish gray. Highlights are denoted by strokes of pure white qualified with pale subdued tints of blue, yellow or raw sienna. Shadows of dark red-violets, pinkgrays and neutralized shades of greenish-blue are very effective.

Other landscape objects are treated in subdued gray tones of their natural colors in order to reduce contrasts. Highlights and shadows are rendered in variations of the identical colors used to represent the snow, thereby maintaining an even color balance throughout the picture.

As noted in the above descriptions, snow studies can be interpreted in many diversified moods. The important factor to remember is that of adhering to one predominating color theme. This may be a gray, pinkish-blue, as in an early morning scene; the greenish-blue suggestive of midday; the blue-gray of a dull, overcast sky; or the blue-violet of the moonlight study. Those are basic dominating colors and influence all other tones used in the picture. By keeping contrasts in a low scale and using subdued cool colors, snow studies will convey a natural realism and most artistic effect.

MOONLIGHT EFFECTS. Many types of sunset scenes, taken with the sun hidden behind the clouds, lend themselves exceptionally well to moonlight color impressions. In order to flood the scene with enough light for practical coloring, the moon, or a representation thereof, should be visible in the picture. This usually means that an artificial moon will have to be inserted by the colorist. The placement of the moon is very important and its location is determined by the reflection on the clouds and the general light source governing the entire scene. A particularly pleasing effect is achieved by keeping the moon partly submerged behind a cloud. Generally, a full moon is placed high in the sky to create the necessary impression of maximum illumination relative to the balance of the landscape.

After the sky has been colored in the usual manner, the spot for the moon is decided upon and the paint removed by the use of turpentine or medium on a cotton pointed skewer. The round spot, or design, representing the moon, is then colored with opaque white and toned down with yellow and a faint touch of the adjacent sky color. In some cases where the moon appears too prominent or artificial, its coloring is subdued and softened around the edges by a slight blending with the sky color. Such a procedure, while it greatly enhances the general effect, must be artistically done to create a natural impression.

Moonlight studies are ordinarily depicted in one of three different color themes; blue; yellow-green; or blue-black. In a picture using a cool blue as the dominating color, the sky and clouds are first given a base of medium blue. In the immediate vicinity of the spot where the moon is to be inserted, the sky takes on a yellowish-green cast produced by blending light yellow over the blue base color. The moon is now inserted and colored as previously described. The yellow-green sky tint, around the moon, is gradually blended into a medium blue in the middle sky and on into a dark blue-violet at the horizon.

Highlights on the clouds are worked with white and yellow toned down with raw sienna and pale green. Violet is imparted to the cloud shadows and blended with dark blue halftones. Far distant objects are practically indistinct by moonlight and are colored with the indefinite deep blue-violet shades of the night sky at the horizon. A body of water, such as a lake, stream or ocean, under such sky conditions, will carry a cool medium blue as its base color with reflected highlights of pale yellow and pinkish-violet. Shadows acquire a dark blue-violet shade intensified with black if necessary.

The understood and natural colors of all other objects in the scene are subdued and influenced by the overall blue-violet color theme of the entire picture. Shadows may be carried out in cold blues, violets and blacks. Highlights are depicted with cool impressions of white tempered with blue or blue-green.

Our second color theme is one which contains a warm yellow-green as our predominate color. The moon is registered in a definite light yellow tint. The neighboring sky takes on a pale yellowish-green blending into a cool blue and violet as the distant horizon is approached. Highlights on the clouds are yellows softened with touches of medium green and crimson. Halftones acquire a decided yellow-green appearance and are blended into the cool blue-violet shadow tones of the clouds. Distant and middle distant objects are practically obliberated in detail and are heavily colored in deep blues and violets. Strong applications of dark brownish-greens are noticeable in the middle distant objects.

Water is rendered in yellowish-green highlights, dark green shadows and deep blue-violet halftones. The balance of the scene is colored with due respect to the overall yellow-green color theme and reflected light of the pale yellow moon. Most all other objects are first rendered in darker tones of their natural coloring with yellow-green highlights, blue and violet halftones and dark brownish-green shadows strengthened with violet and black.

The third color theme is one dominated by the cold blue-black tones of night. Again the moon is colored in a natural pale yellow tint. The adjacent sky blends from a greenish-blue into a medium blue and on into a blue-black shade qualified with violet at the horizon. Clouds pick up semi-cool highlights of pale rose subdued with violet. The halftones are a dark blue-greenish gray and the shadows a definite blue-black with a brownish-green tint. Slight variations of these same colors are carried throughout the entire picture with all highlights, halftones and shadows rendered in the above manner.

Direct moonlight reflections on the ocean, or other bodies of water, are quite intense in color and contrast rendition. These extreme highlights call for bold strokes of opaque white subdued with raw sienna, pale yellow and touches of diluted rose. The semi-shadows of the waves are dark green and are gradually blended into the deep trough shadows of dark blue and violet mixed with black. The lesser highlights, on either side of the moons silvery path, absorb much of the natural blue-green color of the water and are best represented by pale yellows greatly subdued with medium green.

A most artistic and effective finishing touch to moonlight studies is the insertion of a small spot of a bright, warm, vivid color such as red-orange or vermillion and yellow. The light in a house window; an outdoor camp fire; or the port light of a sailing vessel; all are ideal spots for a touch of vivid red. If the color is reflected on the water, the effect is substantially increased. All objects near this bright fire color absorb its reflected light and should have their highlights rendered accordingly with pronounced touches of yellow, orange and vermillion. When properly inserted, this brilliant spot of contrasting color will artistically enliven the entire picture.

Chapter Eleven

MISCELLANEOUS OUTDOOR SUBJECTS

In addition to the various subjects already studied, there are often included in a landscapes composition other objects which naturally require the attention of the colorist. Some of these are of minor importance, while others will represent the center of interest in the pictorial composition. The coloring of these various objects are naturally influenced by the basic fundamentals of coloring plus their relative importance in the picture. Obviously, it is impossible to list the innumerable miscellaneous subjects which are apt to be visible in a photographic landscape but the following list comprises the most common examples encountered in the average scene.

HOUSES and barns in a photograph offer a most opportune spot for the insertion of those brilliant contrasting colors which do so much to stimulate and enliven the entire study. Rustic houses and log cabins ordinarily have that weather-beaten appearance and are given a base color of a rich reddish-brown, or burnt sienna, to represent their light side. Cracks of the logs, or lumber, are shaded with a dark brown while the highlights are carried out in light oranges and yellows. The shady side of the structure, and all other shadows, are worked in a cool brown mixed with a little blue or black. The cool highlights in the shadows acquire a light bluish-gray tint. Reflected pale green tints from the surrounding vegetation, applied to the half-tones, do much to enhance the effect.

COUNTRY HOMES are first colored in their natural painted shades. White or other light colored buildings are exceptionally pleasing with the shutters and other trimmings rendered in a bright color, in contrast with the general color scheme.

BRICK BUILDINGS demand a reddish brown tone obtained by mixing burnt sienna with red and a trace of black. Violet is added for the shadows and bright red or vermillion used in the highlights. The base brick color is rubbed off the mortar and intensified with white where the sunlight strikes the bricks. In the shade, the mortar separations absorb a subdued blue tint.

STUCCO, as a rule, is best represented in a light raw sienna with the intense highlights treated in strong touches of white and pale yellow. Shadows may be built up with the addition of blue and violet. In most cases, even where the stucco is a decided white, the above treatment will produce a warmer result and more pleasing effect. A pure white building may be represented by the white of the photograph paper. But it is important to bring out the whiteness with faint traces of blue in the shadows and yellow and white in the middle tones. The white of the photographic paper has a gray cast and requires the insertion of the two above colors to make the whites appear whiter.

OFFICE BUILDINGS, monuments and similar structures are subjected to a neutral gray tint with shadows of a blue-gray, Paynes Gray, and highlights in bluish-whites. Window glass is treated with a diluted blue or blue-green, Veridian, with white highlights.

IRON and steel structures, such as bridges, trestles, storage tanks and other engineering works, may be colored first with a diluted black or a dark blue gray. Their shadows are accentuated with strong blues and violet. The highlights are cool tints of the reflected sky colors. Rusty iron fences, gates, etc., call for burnt sienna mixed with red or vermillion.

AUTOMOILES. Bringing out the bright coloring of automobile bodies often presents a problem to the student colorist. Many shades of red, maroon, blue, green and brown, when photographed, appear dark gray on the photographic print and refuse to absorb a sufficient quantity of the transparent colors to yield the desired tone. Under such conditions, it is necessary to resort to opaque or semi-opaque color application to produce the proper color value over the dark gray undertones on the original print. The extreme highlights on the automobile body are reflections of the sky colors, or other nearbly objects, and should be treated accordingly.

CONCRETE sidewalks and roads have a decided gray appearance and are best represented with a tint of neutral gray. Warm parts and highlights have a tinge of raw sienna. Cool shady sections are blended with a cool blue, such as ultramarine.

ASPHALT roads respond to much the same treatment except that a trifle more blue with a touch of black is added to the shadows. The highlights are interpreted in a pale blue and warmed up with raw sienna if desired.

DIRT roads and pathways are suggestive of a good clay color, such as a slightly neutralized yellow or raw sienna, with faint blendings of burnt sienna. Yellows and whites are representative of the highlights with sepia an excellent shadow color. The effect will benefit greatly by occasional touches of orange or vermillion.

ANIMALS. Dogs and cats quite frequently are the principal object of interest in a photograph and consequently require careful color rendition. White hair is given a realistic appearance with small incidental strokes of blue-gray, pale yellow-green and white subdued with yellow. The applications of these colors should follow the flow or contour of the hair and evenly blend into the adjacent whites. Black hair is best depicted with a base color of diluted black and then built up with dark blue and violet in the shadows. A pale light violet or blue-violet greatly improves the highlights. Brown hair or fur is rendered with a base color of burnt sienna and lightened with yellow or darkened with black to the desired tone. Dark brown is used for the shadows and raw sienna or subdued yellow for the highlights. Incidental touches of red in the halftones produces a most pleasing effect. White haired animals with black spots have their white parts qualified with tints of blue and violet. Animals with white hair and brown spots have the whites built up by the addition of pale yellows, yellow-greens and strokes of diluted rose madder or carmine.

Cats' eyes are best rendered in a yellowish-green with black pupils. The eyes of most other animals are, as a rule, dark brown with black pupils. Catch lights in the eyes are cleaned out with cotton and medium or added with a touch of white faintly toned down with blue or brown. If an animal's tongue is visible it is painted a bright red. Teeth are colored in a white subdued with raw sienna. Noses are generally black with a touch of warm brown in the middle tones and cool pale blue in the highlights. Horses, cattle, sheep and other animals lend themselves to practically the same coloring procedure as described above.

BIRDS, BUTTERFLIES and colorful insects are rendered in their natural colors as nearly as possible. In many instances, the subject is the center of interest and the coloring should be representative of nature's brilliant, attention arresting tones. Yet, on the other hand, the colors may require considerable toning down in brilliance and tonal value, dependent upon the objects' importance in the general composition.

Innumerable miscellaneous landscape objects will present themselves from time to time. Each should first be tinted in their known colors. Highlights are generally lighter tints of the understood base color and shadows darker shades of the same. The colors of the objects are all affected by the reflected light and each is subdued or intensified with relation to the established color theme of the study. The proper selection of tints and shades, for highlights and shadows, should now come to the colorist with little difficulty. Particularly, if he has absorbed the simple rules set forth in the preceeding examples of landscape coloring.

Chapter Twelve

FLOWERS AND STILL LIFE STUDIES

The photography and painting of flowers, fruit, vegetables, pottery, pieces of art and other inaminate subjects, is known as still life. This chapter will deal principally with flowers and fruit as these represent the most common examples of colorful still life compositions.

FLOWERS. Good flower prints lend themselves to exceptionally beautiful color results. Owing to their vivid color combinations, and in order to render the tints in sufficient brilliancy for both a true and artistic effect, the use of heavy, semi-opaque color applications are most appropriate. Here the importance of careful, smooth, color blending is again emphasized. In order to retain the natural, soft, delicate mood of the flowers' structure, it is imperative that the colors be evenly rubbed down and smoothly blended to produce a true representation of the curved shape and roundness of the object. If bold strokes of heavy color are used they should follow the general contour and shape of the petals, stamens, pistils and stems of the flower and should be discreetly blended into adjacent colors.

Backgrounds in still life studies are best when restrained and subdued as much as possible so that attention may be concentrated on the foreground composition. In many cases, extremely dark backgrounds are most appropriate for floral pictures. If a background is black in the print, it is enhanced by faint blendings of dark brown, violet, green or blue dependent entirely upon the general color theme of the picture. Lighter backgrounds are effective when worked in soft contrasting colors to bring out the lifelike beauty of the flowers. Extreme contrasts should be avoided. It is preferable to adhere to mild, delicate, pastel tints or dark subdued modified shades.

The color, or colors, used in the background are reflected onto the flowers, thereby affecting their tints and shades. For instance, if a background is a dark yellow drape, the dominating yellow tone will be reflected into the highlights and shadows of the flower. Some flower petals have an extremely thin texture and are so translucent that the penetration of the adjacent reflected colors is quite pronounced. Bold touches of white, or extremely paled highlight tints on the edges of the flower petals, imparts the required delicate roundness to the flower and produces a most natural lifelike effect.

In order to keep the colors clear, crisp and bright, it is best to work in the lighter tints first and add the intermediate and shadow tones later. This procedure reduces the possibility of obtaining dull and muddy mixtures. Owing to the fact that each type of flower has its own characteristic color, with each differing from the other, it is practically impossible to describe the actual coloring procedure used in each case. But the following descriptions will list the most common examples viewed in floral compositions and materially help the student in the coloring of all flowers.

RED ROSES. Carmine or rose is an excellent base color. The highlights are lighter tints of carmine or vermillion and white. Shadows are intensified with neutral gray or black and faint traces of blue.

YELLOW ROSES. The base color is a medium yellow with light yellow and white used for the highlights. Shadows are worked in raw sienna and a warm brown with touches of light green or pale blue.

PINK ROSES. Rose Madder or diluted carmine can be used for the base color with white added for the highlights. Tints of blue or violet are effective when blended into the shadows.

Dick Whittington

Close Up of a Rose

The coloring of flowers must be smoothly blended
in order to retain the soft, delicate mood of the
flowers' structure and impart the feeling of roundness
to the object.   See Chapter Twelve.

Portrait of a Blonde

Black and white study used in the step by step
coloring procedure described in Chapter Fourteen.

PORTRAIT OF A BLONDE

This type of subject lends itself to soft pastel
coloring in both draperies and background.

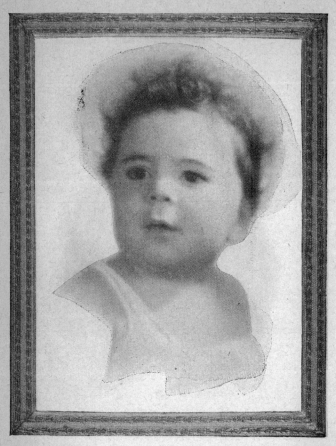

W. J. Seemann

Miniature of a Child

Photographs of babies and children are most appropriately rendered in soft delicate colors in keeping with the subject. Colors are inserted in the background to separate it from the subject thereby creating better perspective.

DICK WHITTINGTON

MINIATURE OF A BRUNETTE

This type of miniature is greatly enhanced by the use of heavy opaque colors in both the draperies and background. In order to maintain an even color balance, the opaque colors must be carefully matched and blended with the transparent applications.

DICK WHITTINGTON

THE CAT AND THE BONE

Plain backgrounds covering large areas are very effective when broken up with several different related
colors applied in a definite pattern or design.

ALLEN L. SUTTER

INDIAN CHIEF

This type of subject is ideal for the use of bright
vivid colors. Much of the fine detail work is best
applied with small brushes using opaque density colors.

DICK WHITTINGTON

SEASCAPE

Clouds require the smooth blending of colors to properly interpret a fluffy and bouyant feeling. The coloring of water is greatly affected by reflected light from the surrounding elements.   See Chapters Six and Seven.

RED CARNATIONS are colored first in vermillion with white or pale yellow added for the highlights. Carmine with a faint tint of black is excellent for the shadows.

DARK RED CARNATIONS are rendered in a mixture of burnt sienna and carmine with pale yellow and white added for the highlights. Neutral gray or black with touches of dark brown strengthen the shadows.

YELLOW CARNATIONS. The base color is a light yellow with white added for the highlights. The shadows take on raw sienna with tints of pale green.

RED POPPIESS. These large field poppies are colored first with vermillion. Highlights are inserted by touches of white and yellow. Blue and burnt sienna is used for the shadows. The poppy centers are black with touches of umber and dark blue.

YELLOW POPPIES. Cadmium Yellow is an excellent base color with shadows brought out by the addition of raw sienna and a yellow orange. Highlights are light yellow and white.

POINSETTIAS. Vermillion is used as the base color. Highlights are yellow and white or a mixture of carmine and white. Shadows are vermillion darkened with Verona brown and touches of dark blue or black. The small seeds in the flower's center are denoted in light yellow with touches of blue or green.

PANSIES are grown in such a variety of colors that it is impossible to list them all. The dark blackish variety can be colored in black mixed with burnt sienna or any of the reds to produce the desired tone. Yellow pansies have dark yellow for their base color with blendings of light yellow and white for the highlights and burnt sienna for the shadows. As a rule, the three dark center spots of the pansy are denoted in black, a dark brown or deep violet.

The following instructions are more or less generalized to cover the tinting of all flowers not previously described. These basic fundamentals used for various color groups will prove of value to the student in the coloring of all flowers. It is understood, of course, that slight variations may be required in the suggested color combinations. These, in most cases, will be governed by the flowers natural coloring and the general color theme of the entire study.

WHITE FLOWERS. Roses, Lilies, Daisies, Gladiolus, Gardenias and other white flowers all respond to practically the same color treatment. Usually a base color of white is used and slightly qualified with a faint touch of black, blue or yellow. Highlights call for pure white with light tints of pink and yellow according to the reflected colors of nearby objects. Shadows are rendered in a subdued yellow, such as raw sienna, or a yellow green with touches of pink. On flowers, like Lilies, a definite green cast is imparted to the lower part of the flower near the stem.

YELLOW FLOWERS. Daffodils, Narcissi, Zinnias, Marigolds, Chrysanthemums, Tritomas, Day Lilies, Asters and other yellow colored flowers range in tones from pale light yellow to a deep golden yellow. Light yellow mixed with white is representative of the pale tints. Highlights are almost pure white with the shadows colored in raw sienna and subdued greens. Pure cadmium yellow is good for the bright vivid yellows and deep cadmium yellow for the darker tones. Highlights range from pure white to lighter tints of the base color. Shadows are depicted in darker shades of the base color with raw sienna, burnt sienna and pale greens used to qualify or intensify the effect.

PINK FLOWERS. Petunias, Asters, Zinnias, Tulips, Geraniums, Roses, Hydrangeas and similar pink flowers range in tints from a pale white pink to a deep violet pink. The pale tints are produced by mixing white and carmine, rose or any of the other reds to render the desired value.

The darker pinks have more red added and strengthened with faint traces of blue or violet. Highlights are white or pale pink. Shadows are darker shades of the base color with blendings of blue, violet or neutral gray.

LAVENDER AND VIOLET FLOWERS. The Iris, Asters, Clematis, Violets, Tulips, Lilacs and other flowers of similar colors are rendered first with their known base color. If a pale lavender tint is needed, use violet mixed with white. If a pinkish violet is required, add a little carmine or rose to cobalt violet. Deep purples are obtained by mixing violet with black or dark blue and then warmed up with burnt sienna or carmine where necessary. Other shades of lavender, violet and purple may be produced by mixing various proportions of blue and red. Highlights are usually lighter tints of the base color with darker shades of the same representing the shadows.

BLUE FLOWERS. Morning Glories, Stocks, Forget-Me-Nots, Delphiniums and other flowers with a predominating blue base color ,are quite varied in their color rendition. The blues will range from the pale violet blue of the Morning Glory to the bright, vivid blue of the Forget-Me-Nots. Ultramarine or cobalt blue is used for the base color and paled with white or darkened with neutral gray to the desired shade. Highlights are a pale blue with the shadows partaking of darker shades of the base color. The shadow effects are enhanced with touches of a red violet.

Remember that all colors are affected by the reflected light from nearby objects. This color reflection is particularly noticeable in the tinting of white or other light colored flowers. The whiteness is intensified by the addition of tints from the neighboring associated colors and helps to bring the whole picture together. The importance of a related balance between foreground and background colors cannot be over emphasized. It is just as essential to the successful color rendition of still life studies as it is in all other types of compositions.

FRUITS, vegetables, plates, baskets and other still life subjects, frequently, make up interesting photographic compositions. These are immeasurably improved by the addition of color. Flowers demand a certain delicate and transparent color rendition to present a lifelike effect. Fruit, vegetables and other objects generally are thick solids and must be colored with this in mind. If the object's surface or skin has a smooth and shiny texture, like plates, polished metal, apples, pears and tomatoes, the highlights are usually bright and intense reflections. These are appropriately denoted in almost pure white subdued only slightly with a touch of the base color. Warm highlights may have the addition of yellow, or interpreted by a bright vivid yellow, as the occasion demands. If the subjects surface texture is somewhat dull or velvety in appearance, the highlights are toned down accordingly.

The same principles and color combinations, used for flowers, may be adapted to the tinting of all still life objects of similar color composition. With a little imagination the student can produce outstanding still life color impressions greatly superior to identical studies in black and white.

Chapter Thirteen

PORTRAITS

Portraits in general respond to much the same coloring principles with only slight variations in the basic flesh tones to represent the particular type of individual portrayed.

In the coloring of portraits, the students' knowledge and understanding of color harmony will prove a most valuable asset. Although the flesh, cheeks, eyes, lips and hair of the subject are governed by fundamental color restrictions, the background, clothing and miscellaneous accessories are dependent, to a large extent, upon the artist's selection of colors for a harmonious effect. Consequently, these subordinate elements play a most prominent part in the final achievement.

It is a known fact that certain hues are more pleasing and becoming to different types of people. Inasmuch as the colors are so varied for each type, it is suggested that the student study the many color reproductions of portraits appearing in national magazines and analyze the numerous colorful combinations used with blondes, brunettes, redheads and other characteristic types.

As a rule, the rotation of colors as applied to a portrait, are first, the base flesh tone, then the cheeks, flesh shadows, lips, whites of the eyes, iris, pupil, flesh highlights, teeth, hair, eyebrows, eyelashes, background, clothing, jewelry and other miscellaneous objects in the proper sequence. The above procedure may be varied according to the colorist's own individual requirements. Some artists prefer to work in the background colors first while others leave it as one of the final steps in the coloring of the photograph.

The latter method provides a better opportunity for the artist to study the nearly finished portrait and choose the appropriate colors and values that best suit the composition. Should it be desirable to insert the background first, the choice of colors must be predetermined and laid on accordingly. If slight changes are necessary, after the balance of the portrait has been completed, they may be worked in as a final step to bring the entire study into harmony.

BACKGROUNDS. The density of the original print has a great influence on the choice of colors selected. A background that is dark and heavy calls for the use of heavier pigments such as brown, orange, red, dark blue, violet and green. Light delicate tints do not impart enough color over the dark grays and blacks of the original dense photographic background to register the proper tones. The lighter density backgrounds lend themselves exceptionally well to soft pastel combinations and it is here the delicate blendings of blues, violets, greens and yellows are most appropriate.

In most cases, analogous, or associated color combinations, are best suited for photographic backgrounds. For example, if a dress is green the background can blend from a soft yellow, at the lower part of the background, through a yellow green and on into a blue green at the top. Or, if the dress is yellow the background can blend from a yellow green through a bright green and into a darker blue green or olive green. Frequently, a touch of contrasting color will improve the effect. In the above examples, yellow is our predominating color. Violet, the contrasting complement of yellow, may be blended into the background and will be in harmony with the other colors.

When using brighter tints keep them confined more to the center of the background with darker and subdued colors used around the very edges of the print. This procedure has a tendency to help the general composition by keeping the attention focused on the main center of interest, the portrait itself.

Children's and babies' portraits are generally extremely light in density, apropos to the delicate nature of the subject. In backgrounds of this type, the colors may be soft and indistinct blendings of faint tints in harmony with the flesh tones or clothing, whichever is the predominating color. White backgrounds should have slightly stronger colors inserted directly around the subject and gradually blended down so as to melt into the white near the edges of the print. This method of color application is pleasing and beneficial to the general composition.

Backgrounds, which seem to crowd the subject, may be pushed back by increasing the contrast between the portrait and the background. Hence, a light baby portrait may be separated from the background by inserting darker colors directly in back of the subject. Likewise, a portrait with dark hair and clothes may be brought out from a dark background by applying lighter colors around the subject. This procedure will impart greater depth and perspective to the study.

Frequently, backgrounds are enhanced by working in a faint pattern or design. This is especially true where the background area is quite large. The design may vary from a soft mottled effect, made up of various harmonizing colors, to one showing visable downward strokes of contrasting shades. Artificial designs in a background must be held down in color value and softly blended with the adjacent tints otherwise they may become conspicuous and lose their effectiveness.

Note how the dark background of the cat picture, page 86, has been enlivened and warmed up by the strokes of burnt sienna, Verona brown and a warm green. Note also, how the immediate foreground rug has been darkened and subdued at the lower part of the photo, thereby directing and holding our attention on the main subject.

Blondes, as a rule, require a background that is soft and delicate with light tinted effects. Portraits of brunettes, however, call for heavier and brighter colors. This type can stand background tones of red, orange, red-violet, green, blue and reddish browns. If dark green or blue is used over large areas it is advisable to warm it up with additions of red or reddish brown, otherwise the flesh tones will appear lighter in density and take on a greenish tint.

FLESH. Different types of people are known for their characteristic complexions, which are more or less individual, and must be taken into consideration by the artist for a natural flesh tone rendition. Blondes are known for their slightly pinkish flesh color, brunettes for their olive complexion, redheads for their decided pink skin. Men usually have a dark swarthy complexion while children's and babies' skin is a delicate, pearly flesh tone. Therefore, it is reasonable to assume that the basic flesh tone of each individual type demands a slightly different color mixture.

The flesh color, which comes with most photo oil sets, may be used as a basic flesh tint for practically all types of complexions but must be altered slightly with red or yellow to suit the individual. For those desiring to mix their own flesh color the following is recommended as it has been used by some of the best portrait and miniature colorists in the country. The basic colors used are Alizarin Crimson, French Vermillion, Indian Yellow and White. For a brunette basic flesh tone, on a light print with weak shadows, a mixture of approximately one part Alizarin Crimson, two parts Indian Yellow and two parts white is used. By adding more of the red and white to the above mixture a good base flesh tone is obtained for blondes and children. A man's flesh tint will take on more of the red and yellow and less white so as to produce a darker shade. The shadow tones in each case are built up with burnt sienna and a touch of the base flesh tone. If a sepia or buff print is used, red should be mixed with the burnt sienna for the shadows and less yellow used in the base flesh mixture.

Dark prints with heavy shadows and deep skin textures have French Vermillion substituted in place of Alizarin

Crimson with a trifle larger quantity of this red used in the flesh tone mixture. The flesh shadows are worked with burnt sienna and red in the dark parts and vermillion and Indian yellow for the lighter shadows. In case the complexion appears too yellow, a light tint of blue will tone it down and render a pleasing delicate tint.

For those using the standard Flesh photo color the same principles will apply. Crimson is added where red is called for and chrome yellow medium with a touch of raw sienna may be substituted for Indian yellow if necessary. The shadow tones should be applied by the same procedure as previously described. Inasmuch as exact proportions of color mixtures cannot be relied upon, it is up to the student to use his own "color sense" in producing the proper flesh tone. The beginner should select outstanding natural color reproductions of each type of complexion and keep these before him at all times as a color guide. This method will help tremendously in acquiring natural flesh tones until experience has been gained.

After the flesh tint has been smoothly rubbed down, the shadows are worked in and evenly blended into the flesh tone.

The flesh highlights may be brought out by slightly rubbing down the base flesh tone or applying a light mixture of flesh and opaque white. This latter procedure is preferable as it tends to build up the flesh tint instead of removing it by the rub off method. The most pronounced highlights will appear on the bridge of the nose, chin, upper lip, corners of the lower lip, forehead, eyelids, corners of the eye, and neck and shoulders of the subject.

CHEEKS. The cheek color should be inserted after the flesh shadows have been worked in. This method of color rotation allows for a truer cheek rendition and smoother blending with the flesh tones. The cheek color may be composed of two parts of the flesh tone and one part of the particular red used in its mixture. In other words, if Alizarin Crimson is the component red used in the flesh mixture, it likewise should be used for the cheek color. The regular

Cheek supplied in photo oil sets is appropriate with slight alterations. A brunette complexion requires a touch of orange to the regular standard Cheek color. The rouged cheeks of a blonde woman may be tinted with Cheek and a touch of the flesh tone. A man's cheeks are generally lighter in color value and are rendered with Cheek, a touch of orange and flesh tint. Children's cheeks, especially babies, take on a decided healthy pinkish appearance and may be handled in practically the same manner as the rouged cheeks of a woman.

A cotton pointed stick is generally employed to blend in the cheek tint. First the cotton is worked with the basic flesh color and then used to pick up just a touch of cheek red. Small circular, half moon strokes are very lightly laid on. Start at the center of the cheek area and gradually blend towards the nose, lower eyelids, ear and lower jaw. By using small circular strokes, carefully blended with the flesh, a most natural skin texture impression is created. Refrain from the use of too much red on the cheeks or an overpaitned, gaudy and unnatural effect will be the result. Overpainted cheeks may be toned down with flesh tint and white.

LIPS. Two different shades of red are most effective in denoting the lip coloring. The upper lip is always a slightly darker shade than the lower and has a dark line separating the two. Women's lips, as a rule, are emphasized with lipstick and partake of a brighter red. The regular Lip tint serves the purpose for the coloring of the upper lip. Cheek or vermillion is added to this color for the lower lip. Highlights are quite intense and interpreted in bright orange or white. By using a little of the basic flesh tone with the lip color a soft lifelike effect is achieved. The dark line separating the two lips is created by adding black or brown to the lip color.

Quite often it is necessary to apply the lip colors in heavy density to impart the proper shade. These semiopaque applications are laid on with a brush using extreme care to follow the exact shape and contour of the lips, otherwise the likeness of the subject may be affected Men's' and children's lips are best represented by the regular basic flesh tone slightly darkened with a touch of the lip color and greatly subdued so as not to be conspicuous. Ordinarily, the lip coloring on these types is just a tone or two darker than the regular flesh tint.

TEETH. First a light tint of cheek with a touch of orange is applied to the gums and inner part of the mouth if visible. The teeth are cleaned of any overlapping color with the aid of a cotton pointed skewer and medium. A good color for the teeth is white faintly subdued with a touch of neutral gray or yellow. The highlights on the teeth may be intensified with spots of opaque white.

EYES. Obviously, the most important element and factor in the portrait composition are the eyes of the subject. The expressive mood and likeness of the subject centers around these prominent centers of interest. Hence, their coloring is of utmost importance in acquiring a realistic impression. When properly done, the eyes will stand out in a radiant lifelike manner which seems to saturate the entire picture with vitality. Because of their prominence in the composition, the artist should carefully study the following coloring descriptions and work with patience in creating the desired and necessary effects.

First the whites of the eyeballs should be cleaned out with a piece of cotton and medium. White, softened with a touch of blue and a tiny trace of flesh, is used as the white eyeball color. This must not be too white or a harsh stary glare will be the result. Next the iris is colored in its natural tint. Light blue eyes are rendered with a mixture of Chinese blue and white with a faint trace of red. Darker blue eyes are represented by a mixture of Chinese blue and Paynes gray. Blue-gray eyes have the iris tinted with Paynes gray. It should be noted that the iris of the eyes have a definite spoke effect radiating from the pupil to the edge of iris. In blue or blue-gray eyes these spokes are denoted with faint strokes of white.

Hazel eyes are first given a blue tint and then burnt sienna added for the iris spokes. Where the eyes appear small in the photograph, the iris may be denoted with a wash of Verona brown and neutral gray for a hazel tint. Light brown eyes have a Verona brown tone with the light portions touched up with white or raw sienna. Dark brown is denoted with sepia and the spoke effect emphasized with the flesh tone.

The iris color may be inserted with a brush or a cotton pointed skewer using extreme care to follow its true outline and shape. The pupil of the eye is colored with Ivory Black and should be inserted with a small brush. The top part of the pupil is usually cut off by the upper eyelid and is actually depicted by a three quarter black circle. A short heavy black line is placed under the lower eyelid, at the top of the pupil, and gradually blended towards the corner of the eye. Black is also used for the rim around the outer edge of the iris, separating it from the white eyeball. A faint touch of orange or vermillion is quite effective when inserted in the corners of the eyes, nostrils and lobes of the ears.

The shadow, in the deep fold over the eyelashes, is colored in a strong burnt sienna and the highlights brought out with white and flesh or by merely rubbing down the base flesh tone. The highlights on the inside of the lower lid also respond to similar treatment. The intense highlight, or catchlight, in the pupil is inserted with a spot of white. Catchlights are absolutely essential to bring out that crisp, lucid, sparkling feeling so necessary for an artistic impression. If catchlights are lacking, it is recommended that they be artificially inserted to enhance the effect.

The eyelashes should be left as the final step in finishing up the eyes. These are, in most cases, worked in with the aid of a brush, using a diluted black or dark brown. The upper lashes are quite pronounced, particularly on women and children. By comparison, the lower lashes are rather indistinct and should be treated accordingly. No attempt should be made to paint each lash as only a suggestion of their growth and natural flow is sufficient.

HAIR. The hair of the subject must receive thoughtful color application in order to bring out the soft wave effects and produce a light fluffy appearance. This is simply accomplished by the proper building up and strengthening of the shadows in relation to the highlights and halftones. For instance, brown hair is first given a basic wash of Verona brown lightly rubbed down. The shadows are built up with sepia and a touch of black. The halftones receive warm touches of burnt sienna laid on next to the highlights. Raw sienna with white and a trifle Verona brown may be used for the general highlights with the intense parts brought out with white, slightly toned down with yellow.

The secret of lifelike hair rendition may be attributed to several factors; the intensification and contrast between highlights and shadows; their gradual blending through the halftones; and the careful stroke technique used in following the general flow of the hair.

When the shadows, halftones and highlights are laid on, with a brush or cotton pointed skewer, fine strokes of each color must follow the contour of the natural hair growth. If the hair appears flat, intensify the shadows with darker colors and lighten the highlights, thereby increasing the contrast between the two. The halftones, between the shadows and highlights, demand a soft gradual blending to impart the feeling of roundness to the hair curls and waves. Definite and visible strokes of color are appropriate, and in fact required, in all parts of the hair to create an artistic effect.

Light brown hair is interpreted with a base tint of raw sienna darkened with Verona brown. Shadows have burnt sienna added while the highlights are rendered in white and raw sienna. Dark brown hair has a base of sepia with black worked into the shadows and Verona brown mixed with white for the highlights. Strokes of burnt sienna inserted in the halftones are most effective.

Black hair may be given a wash of black or neutral gray. The shadows are warmed up with sepia and Verona brown and then intensified with a heavy black. Occasional touches of blue in the deep shadows greatly enhance the effect. Highlights are rendered in white subdued with blue and a faint trace of neutral gray.

Platinum blonde hair has a base tint of Indian yellow or raw sienna mixed with cadmium yellow. The shadows call for burnt sienna and a light Verona brown. Highlights are white and yellow with a touch of vermillion. If the hair appears too greenish, work in a little red to neutralize the colors.

Ash blondes are first given a base tone of raw sienna and the shadows worked with Verona brown and sepia. Touches of burnt sienna are blended into the halftones and the highlights inserted with yellow, orange and white. Reddish brown, hair has a basic tint of vermillion, Indian yellow and white. The shadows are built up with burnt sienna and the highlights intensified with orange and white.

Red hair calls for a base of burnt sienna with the shadows denoted in sepia and Verona brown. Highlights are inserted with yellow, orange and white. Reddish brown, or auburn colored hair, is obtained by a mixture of burnt sienna and sepia. The shadows are sepia and black while the highlights take on burnt sienna and white with touches of orange and yellow.

Gray hair is represented by a light wash of neutral gray and a faint trace of blue. The shadows may be built up with heavier applications of gray and blue, or a Paynes gray. Highlights are rendered in white qualified with either a little blue or yellow. White hair may have its color base represented by the natural tone of the photographic paper or given a faint tint of diluted neutral gray. Shadows are strengthened with neutral gray and a touch of raw sienna. Highlights are almost pure white with a slight softening touch of blue or pale yellow.

The hair line next to the forehead and temples may take on a cold gray appearance after the hair has been colored. To eliminate these cold areas work in more of the base flesh tone warmed up with burnt sienna. Quite often,

faint tints of the background colors are most pleasing
when applied to the hair highlights and halftones which
are nearest the background. These also have a tendency to
produce depth and perspective to the portrait composition.

CLOTHING AND DRAPERY. The true color reproduction
of clothing and draperies is of major importance to the
successful achievement of an artistic result. Quite frequently, the colorist falls down at this point in the coloring procedure undoubtedly assuming that the correct color
rendition of clothing is unimportant.

Different kinds of cloth and textiles possess characteristic draping qualities which must be considered in photo
coloring. Velvet, for example, has soft folds, round edges,
dull reflections and extremely soft shadows. Silk folds acquire sharp edges with strong highlight reflections and
shadows. Light gauze, chiffon and veils, on the other hand,
contain delicate highlights and shadows and owing to their
thin, transparent quality, must show a tint of the objects
color under the drape.

Flat tints of a single color to represent clothing should
be avoided. Variations of tones in both highlights and
shadows are just as important in drapery coloring as in all
other objects of the picture. As a rule, drapery shadows are
denoted by darker shades of the base tone and highlights
depicted in lighter tints of the same. Highlights may be
brought out by a slight rubbing down of the basic color
or adding white with it. The shadows are darkened by adding neutral gray, black or dark brown to the base tone.
Extreme care must be exercised in blending the colors from
the shadows to the highlights. When properly done, the
result will be a gradual transition accurately interpreting
the roundness, depth and richness of the drapery material.

Some colors of draperies require the addition of a contrasting shade or tint in their shadows or highlights. For
instance, a blue drape may have highlights of blue-green
and shadows of violet. Bright green draperies have a touch
of violet in their shadows with yellow added for the highlights. A white dress is represented by the natural tone

of the photographic paper. The shadows have faint tints of pale violet, burnt sienna and pale green. Highlights are brought out with pure white. Many white drapery effects are most pleasing when rendered with blue and yellow in the shadows and halftones.

Lace material is first given a light cream colored wash and then built up with flesh in the shadows and other parts where the flesh shows through. Burnt sienna is worked into the folds and around the outline. The design and highlights are worked in opaque white. Touches of raw sienna, pale violet and blue are very effective.

A most comprehensive list of draperies, jewelry and miscellaneous portrait objects, and the colors used in their interpretation, will be found in the Portrait Color Guide, page 117.

JEWELRY: Beads, necklaces, earrings, brooches, watches, and other pieces of jewelry are best rendered in bold strong touches of color laid on next to one another, thereby creating the necessary vibrant color mood and sparkling vitality essential for a realistic impression.

Pearls, characteristically have a white appearance but actually take on a cream tint in their color rendition. A good base color for pearls is made up of white with a touch of Verona brown. Shadows are blue with touches of yellow to neutralize the blue. Highlights are denoted in spots of white softly blended into the cream base tone.

Yellow gold jewelry is first given a base tint of raw sienna with the shadows built up in burnt sienna. The highlights and reflections are spots of opaque white and pale yellow. An occasional spot of pale blue, laid next to the highlights, snaps up the effect tremendously.

Diamonds and other clear cut stones are depicted in faint delicate tints of several different colors. The shadows are touches of blue, the intermediate tones ranging from a pale yellow to a faint tint of violet pink. The highlights are spots of pure white with incidental touches of pale blue laid next to them.

Platinum and silver objects first receive a base tone of a

diluted blue-gray or Paynes gray. Blue is added for the shadows with the highlights rendered in pure white and touches of blue. The intermediate halftones are extremely impressive with touches of yellow.

Final touches to the portrait study are imperative in order to bring the various elements together in tonal quality and color balance. The flesh shadows, which now appear a trifle gray, may be strengthened with heavier applications of burnt sienna and flesh. The highlights on the face may need further lightening up with flesh and opaque white. If the hands show in the picture, the finger nails will need finishing. Natural, unpainted finger nails are brought out with white and flesh. The edges around the cuticle are emphasized with an outline of burnt sienna. Painted finger nails are rendered in a carmine, or similar red, with white added for the highlights. The hair, undoubtedly, will need the shadows intensified in some parts and subdued in others to bring it into a relative balance with the flesh tones and background.

These final touches each mean a great deal towards the achievement of an artistic and realistic portrait in oils. The indescribable thrill and personal satisfaction that comes to the artist in finishing up a beautifully colored portrait is one of the most pleasant memories the colorist can experience.

Chapter Fourteen

STEP BY STEP PORTRAIT COLORING

In order to acquaint the student with the procedure necessary in the coloring of a portrait, the following step by step description will prove most beneficial and instructive towards achieving a pleasing and artistic result. It is again suggested that the student obtain a portrait sudy similar to our demonstration photograph and actually apply the pigments by the methods herewith described.

On pages 82, 83, will be found the coloring subject of this lesson, a portrait of a blonde woman. One is the original black and white photograph and the other the same picture completely tinted in transparent oils. The first step in the coloring process is to treat, or size, the print with photo Medium or Poppy Oil. This is laid on the print with a piece of cotton, allowed to set for several minutes and then the surplus removed with a clean piece of cotton.

BASE FLESH TONE. The particular print that we have chosen is classified as light in quality containing reasonably light shadows. Consequently, this type of print must have its base flesh tint selected accordingly, namely a mixture of Alizarin Crimson, Indian Yellow and White. An excellent procedure used in the mixing of these colors is to lay them on the palette about two inches apart forming a triangle. The center area is used for mixing by drawing the colors in and mixing as required. If more of any particular color is needed to alter the basic flesh tone they are readily accessible for easy mixing. A small brush is an ideal tool for mixing the colors as it allows for the addition of small, minute quantities of pigment for fine blending.

First, our colors Alizarin Crimson, Indian yellow and white are laid out and mixed as described above by starting with white and adding a little of the crimson and yellow in various proportions for the desired flesh tone. By applying a sample of the color to a piece of plain white paper, or direct to a part of the photograph, the tone can be studied and its mixture altered accordingly. If regular Flesh photo oil color is used it may be mixed with crimson or yellow to yield the proper shade. When the desired flesh mixture has been obtained it is applied to the flesh parts of the photograph with a tuft of cotton using small circular rubbing motions to produce a smooth even tone. The color may overlap into the eyes, hair, dress and background and removed later with clean cotton and Medium.

FLESH SHADOWS. The next step is to work in the flesh shadows. Burnt sienna is an ideal shadow color for this type of print and is applied to the shadow areas with the same cotton tuft used to lay on and blend the base flesh tone. The color is applied quite strong in the darker shadow areas and gradually worked towards, and blended with, the flesh tone. Where the shadows are light, such as on the sides of the nose, around the eyes and ears, a mixture of vermillion and yellow will greatly enhance the effect. These colors may also be employed as an intermediate blending tone between the shadows and highlights. Shadows in small areas are worked in with a cotton pointd stick. The burnt sienna shadow tone is lightly laid on, using small circular strokes to blend the color into the adjacent flesh tint. The shadows around the eyes, in the deep fold of the upper eyelid, under the nose, ear lobes and dimple, were all inserted and blended by this method.

FLESH HIGHLIGHTS. The flesh highlights on the bridge of the nose, over the upper lip, corners of the mouth, chin, forehead, cheek bones and upper and lower eyelids, were all brought out with white slightly subdued with flesh.

These highlights were worked in with a cotton pointed skewer and carefully blended into the adjoining base flesh tone and shadows. Inasmuch as the face of the subject is the main interest in our composition, the highlights are more intense than those on the neck, shoulders and bust. The latter may be termed semi-highlights and are obtained by slightly rubbing down the base flesh tone. Where the underneath photographic gray of the print is too pronounced, the area is built up with white and flesh and applied in the same manner as the highlights on the face. Great care should be exercised in blending the highlights into the adjacent tones and maintaining a relative balance with the halftones and shadows to create the feeling of roundness.

CHEEKS. The cheek color is acquired by adding a little more of the red used in the base flesh tone mixture with a touch of vermillion. This is applied to the cheeks with a cotton pointed skewer. The color is first laid on starting in the center of the cheek area, using light, semicircular strokes. These are gradually worked and blended towards the nose, eyes, ears and lower jaw. Keep the color more intense in the center of the cheek area and lighten the density as it gradually blends into the base flesh tone. The entire effect may be smoothed down by very light blending with the same cotton tuft used on the original base flesh tint. Do not use clean cotton to blend or smooth down any of the delicate flesh tones as it has a tendency to pick up and remove the color from the print. It is always better to use a cotton tuft which has first been worked with the flesh color, thereby eliminating the possibility of removing the flesh color in the blending process. A touch of the cheek color is also inserted in the warm shadows at the corner of the mouth, under the eyelashes, corners of the eyes, on the ears, the light shadows on the neck near the ear, and right shoulder of the subject.

LIPS. Two different reds are used in rendering the lip coloring. The upper lip is first given a wash of crimson

mixed with vermillion and a touch of flesh. The lower lip
is represented with vermillion and flesh. These colors are
applied with a cotton pointed skewer or a small brush, exercising care to follow the exact shape of the lips. The dark
shadow, separating the upper and lower lip, is brought out
by a definite line of Verona brown or dark burnt sienna.
Highlights on the lower lip are quite intense and rendered
with touches of orange and white applied with a brush.

EYES. Now we come to one of the most important parts
of the portrait—the eyes. The whites of the eyes are first
cleaned out with a cotton pointed stick and Medium and
then colored with a mixture of white slightly toned down
with a touch of blue and flesh.

The eye iris is next colored with a mixture of Chinese
blue and white. The pupil is inserted with a brush using
Ivory black. A short black line is added above the pupil,
next to the lower eyelid, and gradually blended towards
the corners of the eyes. The light parts, or spokes, of the
iris are brought out with touches of burnt sienna and a
few incidental highlights of Chinese blue and white. The
rim around the iris, next to the white eyeball, is given a
faint outline of black. The intense highlight reflection, or
catchlight, in the pupils is denoted by a spot of opaque
white applied with a brush. The inside corners of the eye,
next to the nose, are given a most effective touch of light
orange.

After the eyes have been colored this far, it is advisable
to touch up the adjacent highlights and shadows to bring
all the elements into a truer balance. The shadows, under
the lower lid and those in the outside corners of the eyes,
may be intensified if necessary. The deep fold, over the upper lid, is darkened with burnt sienna or Verona brown
using a brush for the application. The highlights, in the
center of the upper and lower eyelids and corners of the
eyes, are emphasized with white and flesh.

The eyes are now completely colored and ready for the
final touch, the coloring of the eyelashes. These are inserted
with a fine brush using Ivory black. Although the lashes

should be quite pronounced they must not be overcolored to the extent of throwing the other elements out of balance. The brush used to insert the lashes should be only lightly charged with paint to secure the proper effect. The upper lashes are always more prominent than the lower lashes and should be treated accordingly.

The eyebrows are next colored with burnt sienna and Verona brown. Fine dark strokes of color, denoting the hair growth, are inserted with a brush carefully following the general flow of the hair. These short fine strokes of dark brown or black create a most natural effect. Practically all the fine detail work, in and around the eyes, is done with small brushes or cotton pointed skewers.

HAIR. The base color used for this particular shade of blonde hair is Indian yellow. The deeper shadows are colored with Verona brown and sepia. The intermediate halftones, next to the highlights, are given a touch of warm burnt sienna and blended into the shadows. The intense highlights, in the front parts of the hair, are brought out with brush strokes of opaque white and yellow. In applying all hair colors use short strokes, each carefully following the contour, swing and natural flow of the waves and curls, thereby creating a realistic impression. Occasional shadow tones, intermingled with the highlights and incidental highlight applications laid in the shadows with a brush, will do much towards an artistic rendition.

The snood on the back of the hair, is brought out with touches of burnt sienna representing the shadows. The glistening highlights are depicted with spots of opaque white, yellow and white, and orange and white. The outer edges of the hair are not finished up until after the background has been colored.

DRESS. The thin, transparent material of the white dress takes on a great variety of colors. A light flesh tint is laid on the dress where the shoulders, arm and chest show through. The shadows, in the dress folds, are rendered in a subdued Chinese blue and Paynes gray. Occasional touches of yellow blended into the halftones are most appropriate and pleasing. The highlights are applied with opaque white, toned down with a trace of blue and are especially pronounced on the edges of the dress folds. These intense highlights are best worked in with a brush using heavy applications of color.

NECKLACE. First a heavy tone of burnt sienna is applied to the necklace. The dark parts, or shadows, are intensified with minute touches of Verona brown. The strong reflected highlights are laid on with a brush in small spots of heavy opaque white. Incidental spots of pale blue, intermingled with the highlight whites, imparts the necessary sparkle to the jewelry and produces a stimulating, vibrant color mood.

BACKGROUND. The colors for the light background have been selected so as to be in harmony with the subject. These colors, pale blue-green and light violet make an excellent combination for a blonde portrait such as this.

A light tint of violet was first blended into the top outside areas of the background. The pale blue-green was worked in around the head so as to increase the contrast, between subject and background, thereby improving the depth and perspective. The blue-green was applied with a large cotton pointed skewer using short downward strokes. These were intentionally laid on in a somewhat careless manner to produce a slight, uneven variation of tones in an otherwise plain background. This semblance of an indistinct design enhances the entire background effect, particularly when the background represents such a large area in the composition.

FINAL TOUCHES. After the background is completely colored, the edges of the hair may be finished. The addition of blue-green in the background may draw some of the yellow out of the flesh tones and make them appear gray. If such is the case, the grayish areas will have to be built up with stronger flesh tones and more yellow. Likewise, if the shadows take on a grayish cast, work in stronger tints of burnt sienna. Any part of the portrait that now appears flat may be enlivened considerably by intensifying the highlights and shadows to produce a stronger contrast. Thus, by adding darker shadows to the hair and then increasing the intensity and tonal value of the highlights, a greater feeling of depth and roundness is acquired. Obviously, the halftones are an important factor as it is this intermediate color which blends and joins the highlights and shadows together for a natural effect. These final touches should not be neglected as it is here the success of the entire coloring mood is determined.

When the job is finished, the white border of the photograph is cleaned of the overlapped color with cotton and turpentine. The picture should then be placed away in a dustless drawer or cabinet and allowed to dry for at least a week before further handling.

After the photograph is thoroughly dry it may be varnished with a protective coating. Special photographic varnishes are made by various photo oil color manufacturers and are available at most art and photographic stores. These are supplied in dull, semi-gloss and high gloss finishes and are easily applied according to the directions of each type. The beauty of the colored print is greatly enhanced by a varnish application. It imparts a pleasing sheen to the photographic surface and seems to bring out and vitalize the colors themselves.

Chapter Fifteen

MINIATURES

Originally miniatures were drawn and painted on ivory with opaque pigments skillfully applied by the artist to render a soft delicate lifelike impression. Photography has tremendously increased the popularity of these small size portraits owing to the simple methods now used in producing them. In the old days the artist had to sketch and paint the likeness onto a blank surface the same as in painting regular portraits in oils. Today, the image is printed onto an ivory-tinted base film coated with a photographic emulsion. Both Ivory and Kotava are manufactured especially for photographic miniatures and are ideal for use with photo oils. In the absence of these, however, the print may be made on regular dull photographic paper and still yield satisfactory coloring results.

A slightly different procedure is followed in the painting of miniatures than that employed to render regular color portraits. Instead of resorting almost entirely to the use of transparent colors, applied by the rub on method, miniatures demand the use of opaque and semi-opaque color applications in conjunction with the regular tinting procedure. In other words, more actual painting is required and less tinting.

Along with the use of heavier color renditions, miniatures respond to a slight overcoloring effect which tends to emphasize the depth and perspective in the tiny composition. This overcoloring is most appropriate for the backgrounds, clothing, drapery, jewelry, hair and other miscellaneous objects in the picture.

The flesh tones should never be exaggerated. These, along with the eyes, eyebrows and teeth, may be depicted with the necessary tints and shades, rubbed on and blended in the usual manner. If the composition demands heavier values, they may be slightly accentuated with intensified colors.

A large magnifying glass and several small artists spotting brushes are necessary implements in the application and blending of the opaque colors and working in the fine details of the eyes, eyebrows, teeth, jewelry, clothing, etc. The miniature is first tinted by the regular method employed in coloring a portrait and then intensified with opaque and semi-opaque pigments. This preliminary tinting will establish the base color theme of each area in the picture and will act as a guide in the proper mixing of the opaque colors. Some miniatures of portraits may require only flesh tones rendered by the customary rub on procedure. Others will demand highlight and shadow intensification with heavy color applications.

Should opaque density colors be employed in the flesh tones they must be carefully mixed to the exact shade of the base flesh color. First the paints are mixed on the palette to the desired shade. The color is then picked up with a brush and laid on the picture with short light strokes. Work both ways from the base flesh tone mixture by using lighter variations for the highlights and darker shades for the shadows. The colors should be lightly applied at first and gradually increased in density until the right effect is accomplished.

The edges of the opaque colors are smoothly blended into the adjoining base tints with a brush lightly charged with a little of the base color. If too much paint is put on it can be removed or toned down with a brush by using small light strokes. Intense highlights and shadows particularly must have their bordering edges blended into the nearby colors with the aid of a dry brush. A little patient practice with fine brushes and opaque mixtures will soon acquaint the student with their proper use and help in attaining proficiency with this important medium in miniature painting.

The hair of the subject is brought out by semi-opaque highlights and shadows appropriately applied and blended into the original base hair tint. Extreme highlight and shadow contrasts should be confined to the front part of the hair. These are toned down as the hair recedes towards the background.

Dresses, clothing and draperies are very important in miniature portrait coloring as it is here the usual necessary richness is imparted to the picture. By resorting to opaque mixtures, the pleasant full bodied rich tones can be acquired—rich tones which do so much to enhance the beauty of the composition. The richness and perspective of the entire study is dependent, to a large extent, upon the coloring of the background and drapery, which, when judiciously applied emphasizes by contrast the soft delicate flesh tones of the subject.

Note the richness imparted to the red velvet jacket in the miniature of the woman, page 85. This was applied in heavy opaque pigments so as to bring out the demanded color and quality of the material. Also note the use of heavy colors in the background and the design inserted for an artistic effect. Backgrounds of this nature are only applicable to miniature coloring as they impart the necessary color impression of a genuine oil painting.

Miniature backgrounds, dark in value, lend themselves to dark, heavy color applications, thereby accentuating by contrast, the soft quality of the portrait. Other backgrounds may be fairly light in value to emphasize a soft, delicate mood, such as in baby studies. See page 84.

SEPIA TONED PRINTS. Sepia toned portraits, or prints on buff paper, are preferred by many professional colorists. The general warm undercoating seems to impart a warm effect to the flesh tones and strengthens the color intensity of the picture without the appearance of overcoloring. The great disadvantage in the use of sepia toned photographs lies in the fact that all colors are materially affected by the warm brown tone. This is particularly noticeable with blue, violet and green color applications. Blue, for instance, when blended with the yellow brown sepia color, will produce a greenish tint. The addition of violet, the complement of yellow, is necessary to neutralize the yellow brown undercoating and intensify the blue.

Owing to this drastic influence on all colors, we do not recommend the coloring of sepia toned prints for the beginner. As experience, in the coloring of regular black and white photographs, is gained and the student becomes thoroughly familiar with the natural rendition of photo colors, he may then experiment with sepia toned prints and determine for himself if the results achieved warrant the use of this medium. It is true that black and white prints contain a coldness which, if not taken into consideration, will produce a somewhat cold effect. However, this is easily counteracted by the addition of warm tints and shades to produce a warm, lifelike color impression.

Chapter Sixteen

PORTRAIT COLOR GUIDE

FLESH TONES FOR WOMEN

BLONDES—Light print with light shadows.

Base Flesh Tone—Alizarin Crimson, Indian Yellow and White
   Or—Regular Flesh with touch of Vermillion.

Flesh Shadows—Burnt Sienna.

Flesh Highlights—Base Flesh Tone with White and Orange.
   Or—Rub down the base flesh tone.

BLONDES—Dark print with dark shadows.

Base Flesh Tone—*French Vermillion, Indian Yellow & White
   Or—Regular Flesh with touch of Cheek.

Light Flesh Shadows—Vermillion with Yellow.

Dark Flesh Shadows—Burnt Sienna and touch of Vermillion.

Flesh Highlights—Add White and Orange to base flesh tone.
   Or—Rub down the base flesh tone

   * Note: If French Vermillion is not available use regular Vermillion with
      touch of Orange.

BLONDES—Sepia or Buff Prints.

Base Flesh Tone—Same as above with less Yellow.
   Or—Regular Flesh with Cheek.

Flesh Shadows—Burnt Sienna with Carmine.

Flesh Highlights—Use White with the base flesh tone

FLESH TONES FOR WOMEN—(Cont.)

BRUNETTES—Light print with light shadows.

    Base Flesh Tone—Alizarin Crimson, Indian Yellow & White.
        Or—Regular Flesh with touch of Vermillion.

    Flesh Shadows—Burnt Sienna.

    Flesh Highlights—White with Flesh and touch of Orange.

BRUNETTES—Dark print with dark shadows.

    Base Flesh Tone—*French Vermillion, Indian Yellow, White
        with touch of Crimson
        Or—Regular Flesh with touch of Crimson.

    Light Flesh Shadows—Vermillion and Yellow.

    Dark Flesh Shadows—Burnt Sienna with Vermillion.

    Flesh Highlights—White with Flesh and touch of Orange.

    Note: If French Vermillion is not available use regular Vermillion with
        a touch of Orange.

BRUNETTES—Sepia or Buff prints.

    Base Flesh Tone—Use less Yellow in flesh tone mixture.
        Or—Regular Flesh with Carmine.

    Flesh Shadows—Use more Red with Burnt Sienna.

    Flesh Highlights—Base flesh tone and White.

GENERAL COLORING FOR WOMEN

Cheeks—Add more of the Red used in the flesh tone mixture.
    Blondes—Cheek with Flesh.
    Brunettes—Cheek or Vermillion with Orange.

Upper Lip—Lip with a touch of Vermillion.

Lower Lip—Vermillion with a touch of Lip.

Lip Highlights—Orange and White.

Nostrils—Lip with Vermillion.

GENERAL COLORING FOR WOMEN—(Cont.)

Lobes of Ears—Lip with Vermillion.

Inside Corners of the Eye—Orange.

Eyebrows—Verona Brown or hair shadow colors.

Eyelashes—Black or hair shadow colors.

Gums and visible parts of the mouth—Cheek with touch of Orange.

Teeth—White toned down with Yellow or Neutral Gray.

Teeth Highlights—White.

Painted Finger Nails—Carmine with White highlights.

Natural Finger Nails—Flesh with White. Highlights—White.

FLESH TONES FOR MEN

OLD MEN, SWARTHY COMPLEXIONS

Base Flesh Tone—Burnt Sienna.
Or—Regular Flesh with Burnt Sienna.

Flesh Shadows—Verona Brown with Carmine.

Flesh Highlights—Raw Sienna or White added to the base flesh tone.

YOUNG MEN

Base Flesh Tone—Alizarin Crimson, Indian Yellow & White.
Or—Regular Flesh with touch of Orange.

Light Flesh Shadows—Vermillion and Yellow.

Dark Flesh Shadows—Burnt Sienna.

Flesh Highlights—Raw Sienna or White added to the base flesh tone.

GENERAL COLORING FOR MEN

Cheeks—Add Vermillion or Cheek to the base flesh tone.

Upper Lip—Lip and Flesh.

Lower Lip—Vermillion or Cheek and Flesh.

Lip Highlights—Orange with White.

GENERAL COLORING FOR MEN—(Cont.)

Corner of the Eye—Orange.

Nostrils and Lobes of Ears—Lip and Vermillion.

Eyebrows—Verona Brown or hair shadow color.

Eyelashes—Black or hair shadow color.

FLESH TONES FOR CHILDREN

CHILDREN—Light print with light shadows.

Base Flesh Tone—Alizarin Crimson, Indian Yellow & White.
    Or—Regular Flesh with touch of Vermillion.

Flesh Shadows—Burnt Sienna.

Flesh Highlights—Add White and Orange to the base flesh
    tone.
    Or—Rub down the base flesh tone.

CHILDREN—Dark print with dark shadows.

Base Flesh Tone—French Vermillion, Indian Yellow and
    White with touch of Carmine.
    Or—Regular Flesh and touch of Carmine.

Light Flesh Shadows—Vermillion and Yellow.

Dark Flesh Shadows—Burnt Sienna and Vermillion.

Flesh Highlights—White with Flesh and touch of Orange.

GENERAL COLORING FOR CHILDREN

Cheeks—Add more of the Red used in the flesh mixture.
    Or—Cheek and Orange.

Upper Lip—Same as Cheek color with more Red added.

Lower Lip—Same as Cheek color with more Orange added.

Lip Highlights—Orange and White.

Nostrils and Lobes of Ears—Lip with Vermillion or Orange.

Corner of the Eyes—Orange.

Eyebrows—Light Verona Brown or hair shadow colors.

Eyelashes—Black or Sepia or slightly darker shade of the hair
    shadow color.

GENERAL COLORING FOR CHILDREN—(Cont.)

Teeth—White toned down with Flesh or Yellow. Highlights—White.

Gums and visible parts of the mouth—Cheek with Orange.

GENERAL COLORING FOR EYES

Eyeball—White subdued with a touch of Blue, Neutral Gray or Flesh.

Highlights—Opaque White.

Pupils—Black.

Catchlights—Opaque White.

Outside Iris Rim—Black.

EYE IRIS COLORS

COLOR OF IRIS	BASE IRIS COLOR	LIGHT PORTIONS AND SPOKES OF THE IRIS
LIGHT BLUE	Chinese Blue & White Faint trace of Red	White with touch of Paynes Gray
DARK BLUE	Ultra Blue and Paynes Gray	White with touch of Paynes Gray
BLUE GRAY	Paynes Gray	White with touch of Blue
GRAY	Neutral Gray	White with touch of Pale Blue
HAZEL	Chinese Blue and White—Touch of Gray	Burnt Sienna & White. Touches of Pale Blue
LIGHT BROWN	Verona Brown	Raw Sienna and White
DARK BROWN	Sepia	Raw Sienna or Flesh

HAIR

COLOR OF HAIR	BASE COLOR	HIGHLIGHTS	SHADOWS
PLATINUM BLONDE	Indian Yellow	Yellow & White Touches of Vermillion	Burnt Sienna & Verona Brown

HAIR—(Cont.)

COLOR OF HAIR	BASE COLOR	HIGHLIGHTS	SHADOWS
ASH BLONDE	Raw Sienna	White and Pale Yellow	Burnt Sienna & Verona Brown
REDDISH BLONDE	Vermillion, Indian Yellow and White	White & Orange	Burnt Sienna & Verona Brown
RED HAIR	Burnt Sienna	Orange, Yellow and White	Verona Brown Sepia & Carmine
AUBURN	Burnt Sienna and Sepia	Burnt Sienna and White. Touches of Orange and Yellow	Sepia and Black
LIGHT BROWN	Raw Sienna and Verona Brown	Raw Sienna and White	Burnt Sienna & Verona Brown
DARK BROWN	Sepia	Verona Brown and White	Sepia and Black
BLACK	Black or Neutral Gray	Neutral Gray & White. Touches of Chinese Blue	Sepia and Black
GRAY	Diluted Neutral Gray with Touch of Blue	White with touch of Blue or Yellow	Paynes Gray or Neutral Gray
WHITE	Diluted Neutral Gray	White with touch of Blue or Yellow	Neutral Gray and Ray Sienna

JEWELRY

KIND	BASE COLOR	HIGHLIGHTS	SHADOWS
YELLOW GOLD	Raw Sienna	White with Yellow	Burnt Sienna
PINK GOLD	Burnt Sienna	White, Orange and Yellow	Burnt Sienna and Sepia
WHITE GOLD SILVER PLATINUM	Diluted Paynes Gray	White with touches of Blue and Yellow	Paynes Gray and Blue
DIAMONDS CLEAR CUT STONES	Diluted Neutral Gray	White with touches of Pale Blue	Blue, Yellow & Violet Pink
WHITE PEARLS	None	White with touches of Blue and Yellow	Neutral Gray and Blue

JEWELRY—(Cont.)

KIND	BASE COLOR	HIGHLIGHTS	SHADOWS
CREAM PEARLS	Raw Sienna	White with Yellow	Neutral Gray and Violet
GARNET	Cerise with touch Violet	White and Cerise	Cerise and Blue. Touches of Verona Brown
AMETHYST	Violet with touch Carmine	White and Violet	Violet and Blue. Touches of Black
EMERALD	Medium Green with Yellow	Yellow & White	Ultra Blue, Dark Green, Verona Brown
RUBY	Carmine	Vermillion and Orange	Carmine, Verona Brown with touches of Neutral Gray
TOPAZ	Orange	Yellow & White	Burnt Sienna & Verona Brown

FLOWERS

(See Page 130)

FURS

(See Page 131)

CLOTHING and DRAPERIES

DRAPE COLOR	BASE COLOR	HIGHLIGHTS	SHADOWS
TAN	Raw Sienna	Yellow & White	Burnt Sienna
MEDIUM BROWN	Verona Brown	Orange & White	Verona Brown with Carmine
DARK BROWN	SEPIA	Orange & White	Sepia with Black & Carmine
BLACK	Black	Rub down or add White	Blue and Black
GRAY	Neutral Gray	White	Paynes Gray with Violet
BLUE GRAY	Paynes Gray	Neutral Gray with White and Blue	Paynes Gray with Ultra Blue

CLOTHING and DRAPERIES—(Cont.)

DRAPE COLOR	BASE COLOR	HIGHLIGHTS	SHADOWS
LIGHT BLUE	Chinese Blue and White	White and Pale Blue	Chinese Blue
MEDIUM BLUE	Chinese Blue	Veridian and White	Ultra Blue with Violet
DEEP BLUE	Ultra Blue	Veridian and White	Ultra Blue with Violet or Rose
BLUE GREEN	Viridian	Viridian, White Touch of Yellow	Ultra Blue with touch of Burnt Sienna
YELLOW GREEN	Oxide Green	Yellow and Oxide Green	Viridian or Dark Green
OLIVE GREEN	Tree Green Touch of Raw Sienna	Raw Sienna with White	Tree Green with Verona Brown
PINK	Carmine and White	White with touch of Carmine	Carmine
LIGHT RED	Vermillion	White & Orange	Lip
MEDIUM RED	Carmine	Vermillion and White	Carmine with Violet
DARK RED	Rose	Carmine & White	Rose with Violet or Blue. Touch of Verona Brown
RED PURPLE	Violet & Rose	Rose Madder and White	Violet
PURPLE	Violet	Rose Madder	Violet with Ultra Blue
MAUVE	Violet and Cerise	Cerise & White	Violet with touch of Blue
BLUE LAVENDER	Violet and Ultra Blue	Violet and White	Violet, Ultra Blue and touch of Carmine
BURNT ORANGE	Orange and Burnt Sienna	Yellow and Orange	Burnt Sienna
ORANGE	Orange	Yellow and Orange	Vermillion
SALMON	Vermillion and Yellow	Yellow with White & Cheek	Vermillion and Orange
PEACH	Cheek, Orange and White	White with touch of Cheek and Orange	Vermillion

CLOTHING and DRAPERIES—(Cont.)

DRAPE COLOR	BASE COLOR	HIGHLIGHTS	SHADOWS
LIGHT YELLOW	Cadmium Yellow and White	White	Medium Yellow
MEDIUM YELLOW	Medium Yellow	White & Yellow	Yelliow with Orange
DARK YELLOW	Medium Yellow with Orange	Yellow & White	Orange
WHITE	None	White	Neutral Gray, Blue and Raw Sienna
GOLD LACE	Raw Sienna	Yellow & White	Burnt Sienna

Chapter Seventeen

LANDSCAPE COLOR GUIDE

On the adjoining pages will be found a most comprehensive list of subjects and their suggested color rendition. This color guide has been simplified and generalized so as to meet practically all requirements in the tinting of landscape and still life studies. Both the beginner and advanced colorist will find this chart of great assistance and inestimable value in the artistic coloring of photographs with transparent oils.

No attempt has been made to list the proportions of each color in a mixture, such as so many parts of one color and so many parts of another. This would be impractical for general purposes inasmuch as each particular scene requires certain variations to achieve the desired effect.

It will be noted that highlights frequently call for the use of white. This does not imply that the addition of white is an absolute necessity. In some cases, the desired highlight effect is achieved by simply rubbing down the base color. In others, a diluted tint will prove satisfactory. But it will be found that a mixture of white is often required to render the highlights in their true values.

If the artist does not have the recommended color at his disposal, a substitute color may be selected from the Photo Oil Color Guide on page 133.

LANDSCAPE COLOR GUIDE

SKIES

SUBJECT	UPPER PART	MIDDLE PART	HORIZON
BLUE SKY	Ultra Blue	Light Chinese Blue	Pale Blue with touch of Rose Madder
HAZY SKY	Blue with Neutral Gray	Pale Chinese Blue with a little Green	Add faint tint of Carmine
WINTER SKY CLEAR DAY	Medium Blue with Raw Sienna or Rose Madder	Add more Raw Sienna	Add Rose Madder, Carmine or Violet
SUNSET SKY CLEAR DAY	Ultra Blue with Paynes Gray	Chinese Blue with Light Yellow or Raw Sienna	Medium Yellow to Vermillion
SUNSET SKY WINTER SNOW SCENE	Blue and Neutral Gray with tint of Green	Light Yellow with Green Tint	Yellow Orange to Vermillion
MOONLIGHT SKY	Pale Yellow Green	Medium Blue Gray with Violet	Blue Violet and Black

CLOUDS

SUBJECT	BASE COLOR	HIGHLIGHTS	SHADOWS
CLOUDS CLEAR DAY	Raw Sienna and Neutral Gray with Rose Madder	Pale Yellow or White with tints of Rose Madder	Light Violet to Blue Gray
STORM CLOUDS DULL DAY	Diluted Neutral Gray	Pale Yellow and White. Touches of Vermillion	Dark Gray, Raw Sienna and Vermillion. Blue Gray with Violet
CLOUDS WINTER SNOW SCENE	Raw Sienna with pale Violet	Raw Sienna and White. Touches of light Green	Diluted Rose Madder to light pinkish Violet
CLOUDS AT SUNSET	Blue Gray with tint of Green	Yellow with White and Vermillion	Red Orange to dark Violet
CLOUDS MOONLIGHT SKY	Viridian with Neutral Gray	Pale Yellow Green. Touches of Carmine	Dark Blue Gray with Violet and Carmine

WATER

SUBJECT	BASE COLOR	HIGHLIGHTS	SHADOWS
OCEAN WATER CLEAR DAY	Ultra Blue	Light Blue, pale Green with tint of Pink Violet	Dark Blue, Violet, Greenish Brown
OCEAN WATER HAZY DAY	Viridian	Diluted Viridian, Light Green, Violet-Red with White	Viridian with dark Blue and Violet. Tints of Green, Brown
OCEAN WATER AT SUNSET	Viridian with Paynes Gray	Light Yellow Orange, Pale Green and Blue with White	Dark Blue, dark Green, deep Violet and Sepia
SUNLIGHT REFLECTIONS ON WATER	Yellow	Yellow and Orange with White	Blue Green, Yellow Green. Touches of Verona Brown
MOONLIGHT REFLECTIONS ON WATER	Yellow	White subdued with Raw Sienna and Green	Yellow Green with Dark Blue
MOUNTAIN LAKES	Ultra Blue	Diluted Blue, Violet and White	Dark Blue with touches Violet and Dark Green
RIVERS STREAMS LOWLAND LAKES	Viridian	Yellow Green. Touches of Verona Brown	Dark Green and Sepia. Touches of Blue
WATERFALLS	White with touch of Blue	White, intensified with light Yellow, Rose and Blue	Blue, Violet and Medium to Dark Green

TREES AND FOLIAGE

SUBJECT	BASE COLOR	HIGHLIGHTS	SHADOWS
OLIVE GREEN FOLIAGE	Tree Green	Raw Sienna, Yellow with pale Olive Green	Tree Green with Brown and Neutral Gray
BLUE GREEN FOLIAGE	Viridian	Olive Green and White. Touches Blue and Raw Sienna	Dark Green, Blue, Violet & Vernon Brown
BROWNISH GREEN FOLIAGE	Tree Green with Raw Sienna	Light Green with Raw Sienna, Yellow & White	Dark Green, Verona Brown and Sepia

TREES and FOLIAGE—(Cont.)

SUBJECT	BASE COLOR	HIGHLIGHTS	SHADOWS
YELLOW GREEN FOLIAGE	Oxide Green	Yellow Green and White. Diluted Raw Sienna & Yellow	Dark Green with touches of Burnt Sienna
AUTUMN FOLIAGE	Burnt Sienna	Yellow, Yellow Orange & White	Orange, Warm Brown & Carmine
TREE TRUNKS WITH HEAVY BARK	Sepia	Raw Sienna, Gray and Violet with White	Burnt Sienna, Blue, Violet and Black
TREE TRUNKS WITH SMOOTH BARK	Neutral Gray with Raw Sienna	Diluted Raw Sienna & White	Sepia, Blue and Violet

ROCKS AND MOUNTAINS

SUBJECT	BASE COLOR	HIGHLIGHTS	SHADOWS
MOUNTAINS WITH FOLIAGE	Tree Green with Raw Sienna and Brown	Diluted Raw Sienna, White with Light Green	Green, Neutral Gray and Brown with Blue and Violet
DESERT MOUNTAINS	Raw Sienna with Burnt Sienna	Raw Sienna, White, Light Yellow	Sepia, Warm Brown, Blue and Violet
DISTANT MOUNTAINS	Diluted Blue, Violet with Neutral Gray	Light Raw Sienna, Pale Blue, Green and Gray	Dark Blue, Violet and Gray. Touches of Raw Sienna
GRANITE PEAKS	Light Blue Gray	Pale Pink Violet Touches of Raw Sienna	Blue, Violet with tints of Brownish Green
WARM GRAY ROCKS	Neutral Gray with touch Raw Sienna	Pale Raw Sienna, White with Light Green	Verona Brown & Green. Touches of Blue, Violet
COLD GRAY ROCKS	Neutral Gray	Diluted Gray, White and Blue	Dark Gray, Blue and Sepia
WARM BROWN ROCKS	Burnt Sienna with Verona Brown	Light Raw Sienna, Yellow and White. Touches Burnt Sienna	Sepia, Green Touches of Violet
SEA ROCKS	Verona Brown	Raw Sienna, Light Yellow, Orange, Blue and White	Sepia, Blue, Violet, Brownish Green

SAND

SUBJECT	BASE COLOR	HIGHLIGHTS	SHADOWS
SAND DUNES	Raw Sienna	Diluted Raw Sienna, Pale Yellow	Sepia, Verona Brown, touches Blue & Violet
WET BEACH SAND	Sepia	Raw Sienna	Sepia and Blue
DRY BEACH SAND	Raw Sienna	Pale Raw Sienna, Yellow with White	Sepia. Touches Burnt Sienna, Blue and Violet

FIELDS

SUBJECT	BASE COLOR	HIGHLIGHTS	SHADOWS
FIELDS GREEN GRASS	Oxide Green	Light Yellow	Viridian, Blue, Dark Warm Brown
FIELDS DRY GRASS	Burnt Sienna	Diluted Raw Sienna, Yellow and White	Verona Brown and Violet
FIELDS PLOUGHED EARTH	Raw Sienna	Diluted Raw Sienna & White	Burnt Sienna with touches of Vermillion

SNOW

SUBJECT	BASE COLOR	HIGHLIGHTS	SHADOWS
SNOW EARLY MORNING	White with trifle Blue and Carmine	White subdued with Yellow, diluted Rose Madder	Blue, Violet and diluted Carmine
SNOW AT MIDDAY	White with faint trace Blue and Violet	White subdued with Light Blue, Yellow, Raw Sienna	Violet with Carmine. Neutral Gray and Blue Green
SNOW AT SUNSET	White with Yellow and touch of Carmine	White subdued with Yellow, pale Green & Carmine	Blue, Violet and Neutral Gray

FLOWERS

SUBJECT	BASE COLOR	HIGHLIGHTS	SHADOWS
WHITE FLOWERS	White with touches of Blue or Raw Sienna	White with pale tints of Pink and Yellow	Raw Sienna, Pale Yellow Green & Pale Carmine

FLOWERS—(Cont.)

SUBJECT	BASE COLOR	HIIGHLIGHTS	SHADOWS
YELLOW FLOWERS	Yellow	White or light tints of Yellow	Raw Sienna and Pale Green
PINK FLOWERS	Carmine and White	White and Pale Pink	Darker tint of base color with Blue and Violet
LAVENDER FLOWERS	Violet and White	White with touch of Violet	Cobalt Violet with Blue or Carmine
PURPLE FLOWERS	Violet, Dark Blue & Carmine	Light Violet or Carmine with White	Black, Burnt Sienna and Blue
BLUE FLOWERS	Blue	White with touch of Blue	Dark Blue and Neutral Gray
RED FLOWERS	Carmine	Carmine with White	Carmine and Neutral Gray. Touches of Blue
DARK RED FLOWERS	Burnt Sienna and Carmine	Carmine paled with Yellow and White	Neutral Gray, Black. Touches of Verona Brown

ANIMALS

SUBJECT	BASE COLOR	HIGHLIGHTS	SHADOWS
WHITE FUR	White with touch of Blue	White intensified with touches Pale Yellow and Blue	Blue Gray, Pale Yellow Green
BLACK FUR	Diluted Black	Light Blue and Pale Violet	Dark Blue, Violet and Black
LIGHT BROWN FUR	Raw Sienna with Burnt Sienna	Diluted Raw Sienna & White	Verona Brown
RED BROWN FUR	Burnt Sienna	Raw Sienna, Orange & **White**	Sepia and Verona Brown with Red
DARK BROWN FUR	Verona Brown	Raw Sienna	Sepia and Black

MISCELLANEOUS OBJECTS

SUBJECT	BASE COLOR	HIGHLIGHTS	SHADOWS
RUSTIC HOUSES AND CABINS	Burnt Sienna	Light Yellow and Orange. Raw Sienna	Sepia, Blue Neutral Gray

MISCELLANEOUS OBJECTS—(Cont.)

SUBJECT	BASE COLOR	HIGHLIGHTS	SHADOWS
RED BRICK BUILDINGS	Burnt Sienna with Carmine	Yellow and Vermillion	Verona Brown and Violet
STUCCO	Diluted Raw Sienna	White and Pale Yellow	Neutral Gray Blue & Violet
MONUMENTS STONE BUILDINGS	Paynes Gray	Diluted Paynes Gray & White	Neutral Gray Blue and Violet
WINDOW GLASS	Diluted Blue	White with touch of Blue	Viridian and Neutral Gray
IRON AND STEEL STRUCTURES	Blue and Neutral Gray	Light Blue, Yellow & White	Paynes Gray Neutral Gray and Violet
RUSTY IRON	Burnt Sienna with Carmine	Yellow and Vermillion	Verona Brown
CONCRETE SIDEWALKS ROADS	Neutral Gray	Raw Sienna or diluted Gray	Blue Gray, Blue and Violet with Neutral Gray
ASPHALT ROADS	Neutral Gray	Diluted Gray with touch Raw Sienna or Light Blue	Paynes Gray Blue and Black
DIRT ROADS AND PATHWAYS	Raw Sienna	Diluted Raw Sienna, Pale Yellow & White	Sepia and Burnt Sienna
WOOD FENCES	Raw Sienna	Pale Raw Sienna, Yellow & White	Sepia, Verona Brown or Burnt Sienna

Chapter Eighteen

PHOTO OIL COLOR GUIDE

The following list is representative of twenty-one standard photo oil colors on the market today. Under each of these major classifications will be found a list of alternate or substitute colors.

In order to simplify and generalize this list for all practical purposes and keep it confined to a minimum group of classifications, a certain amount of tolerance must be expected. It is not implied that the alternates are exact matches for the major color of each group. These will vary according to the conditions under which they are used, the types of paper, method of application and manufacturer's specifications. In many cases, the pigments will show slight variations not only in shade but also strength. This is even true with colors bearing identical names but manufactured under different trade standards.

Frequently the variation in tone is practically negligible. But even where the difference is faintly noticeable, the colors are so closely related to one another in their composition and reproduction that they may, for all practical purposes, be used as a substitute without affecting the final color result.

This guide will prove invaluable to both student and professional as it enables one to instantly select any tint or an alternate from the colors at his disposal.

STANDARD PHOTO OIL COLORS
And Possible Alternates

TREE GREEN
Olive Green

*MEDIUM GREEN
Chrome Green Medium
Chrome Green No. 2
Sap Green

*VIRIDIAN
Viridian Green
Dark Green
Chrome Green Dark
Chrome Green No. 3

CHINESE BLUE
Milori Blue
Prussian Blue
Dark Blue
Cerulean Blue

*ULTRAMARINE BLUE
Ultra Blue
Cobalt Blue
New Blue
Permanent Blue
Sky Blue

CERISE
Geranium Lake
Crimson Lake

*CARMINE
Rose
Rose Madder
Alizarin Crimson
Lip
Rose Carthame
Harrison Red

*MAGENTA (Red Violet)
Following Mixture:
1 pt. Cobalt Violet
1 pt. Carmine

*COBALT VIOLET
Violet
Mauve
Permanent Mauve
Violet Carmine

*NEUTRAL TINT
Neutral Gray
Neutral
Gray

PAYNES GRAY
Serge Blue

*CADMIUM YELLOW
Yellow
Yellow Ochre
Aureolin
Yellow Lake
Canary Yellow
Chrome Yellow Lemon
Chrome Yellow Light
Chrome Yellow Medium

RAW SIENNA
Roman Ochre
Golden Ochre
Yellow Ochre

*CADMIUM YELLOW DEEP
Following Mixture:
1 pt. Yellow
1 pt. Orange

*CADMIUM ORANGE
Orange
Chrome Yellow Orange
Chromium Orange

BURNT SIENNA
Warm Brown
Flesh Ochre

*CHEEK
Scarlet
Vermillion
Scarlet Lake
Cheek Pink

INDIAN RED
Flesh Shadows Warm
Venetian Red
Brown Madder
Flesh No. 3

VERONA BROWN
Burnt Umber
Flesh Shadows Cool

SEPIA
Raw Umber
Van Dyke Brown

*OXIDE GREEN
Chrome Green Light
Permanent Green Light
Chrome Green No. 1

* These colors reproduced in "Photo Oil Color Chart" and "Color Harmony Chart" Pages 10 to 13.

(2)